THE BEST!

Yankees Bring
the World Series
Title Back Home

NEW YORK POST   TRIUMPH
BOOKS

This book is available in quantity at special discounts for your group or organization. For further information, contact:
Triumph Books
542 South Dearborn Street
Suite 750
Chicago, Illinois 60605
(312) 939–3330
Fax (312) 663–3557
www.triumphbooks.com

Printed in U.S.A.
ISBN: 978-1-60078-385-2

Design and page production by Mojo Media Inc.
Joe Funk: Editor
Jason Hinman: Creative Director

Photos by *New York Post* Photographer: Charles Wenzelberg
Photo Editor: Evelyn M. Cordon

Contents

Introduction

November 5, 2009 • By By Mike Vaccaro

Alex Rodriguez didn't want to celebrate prematurely, he knows better, but he couldn't help himself, couldn't keep his arms from flying in the air and his mouth from opening wide, couldn't keep the roar from spilling out of his heart and through his tongue and into the frosty New York night. Not now. He watched the baseball bound along on the ground toward second base, saw Robinson Cano scoop it up, flip it to first baseman Mark Teixeira, and now it was OK to act however he pleased. He'd seen this final act on television many times before, but it had always been someone else's party, someone else's celebration.

And now it was his. Now it was theirs. Now it was time for the New York Yankees to gather at the pitcher's mound and jump for joy and join their fans in an explosion of noise and happiness that would spill out of Yankee Stadium and fill five boroughs and beyond. The scoreboard was frozen forever—Yankees 7, Phillies 3—and so were the results of this 105th World Series: Yankees 4, Phillies 2. For the 27th time, the Yankees would finish a baseball season on top of the sport and on top of the world.

And for the first time in his career, Alex Rodriguez would be a part of it.

"I can't tell you how much this means, to be a part of a team comprised of so many great players and so many good people," Rodriguez would exclaim soon enough, outside the Yankees clubhouse, his hair a sticky mess of champagne and beer, his uniform a sweaty mess, his face a picture of relief and triumph. "I've never been around a better group of guys, ever. We've had such a long journey and we've stuck together since Day One."

And he meant that literally, too.

THE FIRST TIME they'd all gathered in public, there was no champagne, and there were no hugs, and there were very few smiles. This was the morning of February 17, and the every member of the Yankees had filed into a tent behind the right-field line at Steinbrenner Field. They weren't there to hear a preseason pep talk from their manager, or to receive fire-and-brimstone marching orders from their owners. No, they were there as spectators to a spectacle, silent observers to the ordeal of their highest-profile teammate. Quietly they stood off to the side as Alex Rodriguez took his place at a dais-like table, in front of a microphone, and confirmed the worst-kept secret in the city and the sport: he had taken performance-enhancing drugs. The story had broken a few days before. Now he was here for a public confession.

"We knew we weren't taking Tic-Tacs," Rodriguez famously said. "I'm here to take my medicine. After today I hope to focus on baseball. We have a very special team here."

Soon enough, he would discover just how special. But first, there would be another difficult bit of news, there would be discomfort in his hip once he reported to the Dominican Republic's training camp for the World Baseball Classic, and there would be a flight to Colorado and the diagnosis of an injury that at first looked to sideline him for much of the season. One more time, Rodriguez was shrouded in turmoil and his teammates were left to answer for it.

"We will miss him, because how do you not miss a great player like that?" catcher Jorge Posada said on the day Rodriguez had what was termed a "successful" procedure by renowned surgeon Dr. Marc J. Philippon. "Injuries happen in this game. It's on everybody else to pick up the slack."

And that was more likely for the Yankees than it might have been for others, because there'd been such an influx of talent to a clubhouse that already boasted Posada, Derek Jeter, Mariano Rivera and Andy Pettitte, the four surviving members of the Dynasty Boys who'd won four titles in the five years from 1996–2000. In the offseason the Yankees had spent $450 million

to sign CC Sabathia as the ace of their staff, A.J. Burnett as the No. 2 and Mark Teixeira as the starting first baseman. An offseason trade had brought Nick Swisher in from Chicago.

"I think we're a team with balance, and balance is what gets you through the rough spots," said Yankees manager Joe Girardi, whose maiden campaign had yielded the first playoff-free season since 1993 and who entered 2009 with as much to prove as anyone. "And any team, no matter how talented, will have rough spots, and will struggle."

And the Yankees did struggle. Chien-Ming Wang, who'd twice won 19 games in 2006 and 2007, was awful from the start, and suddenly what was looked upon as a lock-down rotation was less so. Joba Chamberlain experienced more growing pains in his first full year as a major-league starter. Xavier Nady, the starting right fielder, went down with a season-ending elbow injury. And Teixeira, got off to a brutal start, spending most of April below .200 and feeling the pinch of missing Rodriguez behind him in the batting order. The Yankees even lost their first-ever game at the

new Yankee Stadium to the Indians on April 16, and two days later fell to the Tribe by the unsightly score of 22–4. It wasn't the start anyone envisioned.

And then, on the evening of Friday, May 8, with the team in Baltimore and sitting at 13–15, languishing in third place, something interesting happened: Rodriguez returned, far sooner than anyone could have hoped when he'd left. He spoke of focusing exclusively on baseball.

"I'm done letting other things distract me," he said.

And in his first swing of the season, Rodriguez crushed a home run off Orioles' starter Jeremy Guthrie. And it was as if a switch had been flicked on the season. Sabathia threw a shutout that night. Almost immediately, Teixeira went from an automatic out to where, by August, he would be discussed as a legitimate MVP candidate. The Yankees developed a lineup that would terrorize even the offense-heavy American League, and they would build an almost scary late-game toughness. The Twins visited the Bronx a few weeks later and in three straight games the Yankees

won in walk-off fashion. That became as much trademark of this team as anything, and soon each walk-off would be punctuated by a cream pie being smushed into the face of the hero du jour by Burnett. They would also pass around a faux championship belt after big wins, an increasing sign that not only did these players play well together, they liked playing well together.

"We really get along, so many of us," said Swisher, whose idea the belt had been. "It makes coming to work every day an incredible experience."

Still, as well as the Yankees were playing, as clear as it seemed they were jelling, there was one looming problem: for the longest time in 2009, they had no idea how to beat their biggest rivals. The first eight times they played the Red Sox, they went 0–8, losing in excruciating fashion a couple of times, in blowouts a couple of times and all manner in between. They fell as far as five games behind the Sox in late June, but took advantage of a post-All-Star-break Sox slump (that coincided with their own streak of eight

straight and 10 out of 11) to creep 2½ games ahead of the Sox when Boston visited Yankee Stadium for games starting August 6. A convincing 13–6 blowout (that also marked John Smoltz' final start for Boston) finally got the Yankees off the schneid. And the next night, at the climax of a tense, taut pitchers' duel that was still scoreless in the 15th inning, Rodriguez clubbed a long home run off Boston's Junichi Tazawa, giving the Yankees a 2–0 victory.

And that, in essence, won the American League East for the Yankees. They swept the four-game series. After starting out 0–8 against the Sox they would win nine of the final 10 meetings.

"In retrospect," Girardi would say in late September, "that might have been the biggest hit we had this year, and the biggest victory. After that, I think we realized just how good we could be."

BY THEN, THE Yankees were the clear-cut favorites to win a championship, and they played like it. Against Minnesota in the AL Division Series, there was but one scare, a two-run deficit in the

Andy Pettitte was the hero on the mound in one of his typical grind-it-out performances for the Yankees.

ninth inning of Game 2 at Yankee Stadium, a deficit erased with one swing of Rodriguez' bat. It was the first harbinger of what would be a watershed postseason for Rodriguez, a player who'd been bottled up so many times in so many previous postseasons. But Rodriguez would be unleashed in this one. Two days later, in Game 3, he hit another homer to turn a 1–0 Twins lead into a tie game. A week later, Game 2 of the A.L. Championship Series against the Los Angeles Angels of Anaheim, he would do it again, clubbing a Brian Fuentes fastball over the wall to tie another game the Yankees would eventually win. And his remarkable season of redemption would be capped in the World Series, when his two-run homer helped turn Game 3 around against the Phillies, and his ninth-inning double would break a Game 4 tie and put the Yankees on the doorstep.

Through it all, he learned to enjoy baseball again, singing a familiar mantra game after game, week after week.

"All I want to do is play," he said. "I enjoy this team, I trust my teammates. In the past I've taken too much on myself and I think I've been a lesser player for it. I just try to keep it simple. I swing at strikes, if I have to pass the baton I pass the baton. And it's worked for me."

In many ways, shockingly, Rodriguez almost became over-looked as the Yankees season grew more successful. Sabathia won the MVP of the ALCS, even though Rodriguez had posted staggering numbers in just about every game. And Hideki Matsui would win the MVP in the World Series after exploding for 6 RBIs in the Game 6 clincher, hitting .615 overall in what may well turn out to be his final game as a Yankee.

"How great is that?" Rodriguez said, genuinely happy for his teammate, and for his team. And, oh yes: happy for himself, a member of that team.

Just one of 25.

One of 25 champions who brought a championship back home. ■

Hideki Matsui had some of the biggest hits in his monstrous career, knocking in six RBIs, in Game 6 of the World Series.

Phils leave Bombers playing from behind

October 28, 2009 • By George A. King III

Cliff Lee's evil arsenal and control good enough to consistently hit a gnat's backside combined with Chase Utley's biceps to put the Yankees in a World Series ditch last night in Game 1.

Lee handcuffed the high-powered Yankees lineup across nine innings, turning it into "The Dead Bat Society," and Utley homered twice off CC Sabathia to lead the Phillies to a 6–1 victory witnessed by a Yankee Stadium crowd of 50,207 that had nothing to get excited about.

"You have to tip your hat to the other guy," Yankees pitching coach Dave Eiland said. "That's the best pitching performance we have seen all year."

Lee went the distance, gave up an unearned run in the ninth, didn't issue a walk and fanned 10. He is 3–0 with a 0.54 ERA in four postseason starts.

"He pitched really well; if he is going to pitch like that, you aren't going to score many runs," said Mark Teixeira, who fanned twice.

Especially when your three, four and five hitters go a combined 1-for-12 with the hit being a one-out single by Jorge Posada in the second inning.

"He threw the ball to both sides of the plate," said Alex Rodriguez, who went 0-for-4 and fanned three times in his first World Series game. "CC pitched well enough to win. We didn't swing the bats well."

Billed as a matchup of lefty aces who are close friends and former Cleveland teammates, Lee delivered a gem. And while Sabathia wasn't bad, he wasn't satisfied.

"We lost, and I didn't pitch well; I had three walks, and I was behind everybody pretty much the whole game," said Sabathia, who gave up two runs and four hits in seven frames. "That's not the way you pitch in the postseason."

Utley homered into the right-field seats on a 3–2, 95-mph fastball in the third and crushed a 96-mph, 0–2 heater into the right-field bleachers in the sixth for the defending World Series champions. They were the first two homers to a lefty given up by Sabathia at Yankee Stadium this year.

Game 2 is tonight, when longtime enemy Pedro Martinez, who put on an entertaining show in the interview room yesterday, throws against A.J. Burnett. Lee's complete-game gem kept the shaky Phillies bullpen out of play. Three of the six Yankees' hits belonged to Derek Jeter.

"Winning Game 1 is huge; it's a seven-game series, and getting that first one out of the way is big for us," Lee said. "Now we've got a chance to take both of them and go into Philly in a real good spot."

Lee lost the shutout in the ninth thanks to a Jimmy Rollins' throwing error while attempting to turn a double play.

After walking Rollins and Shane Victorino to start the eighth inning and continue a shaky postseason, Phil Hughes was lifted for lefty Damaso Marte and received a smattering of boos on the way to the dugout.

Marte fanned Utley and retired Ryan Howard on a fly to right. David Robertson surfaced to face Jayson Werth with runners at the corners. A four-pitch walk loaded the bases for lefty-swinging Raul Ibanez. With lefty Phil Coke not throwing in the pen, Robertson gave up a two-run ground single that hiked the Phillies' lead to 4–0.

Two runs off Brian Bruney in the ninth accounted for the final two tallies.

The Yankees led the majors in walks (663) during the regular season, but Lee didn't issue a free pass. It was the fourth game this year—including the postseason—that the Yankees didn't draw at least one walk.

Asked what tonight's Game 2, means, Rodriguez said, "It's big. We need to win obviously and take it to Philly 1–1, and it's a seven-game series. Today was a tough one." ■

Andy Pettitte and the Yankees could only watch as Cliff Lee outdueled CC Sabathia in a battle of the aces in Game 1.

The CC Factor

October 28, 2009 • By Joel Sherman

Joe Girardi has so many moving parts with his rotation in this World Series. He has to decide whether Chad Gaudin, a $100,000 August pickup, was worthy of starting a Fall Classic game for the $200 million Yankees. He had to contemplate what pitching on three days' rest might mean to A.J. Burnett's head and Andy Pettitte's arm.

But the backbone to support Girardi in all of his decision-making was that CC Sabathia would outpitch Cliff Lee, possibly as many as three times. The Yankees had maneuvered through the first two rounds of the playoffs because Sabathia had set the tone by winning openers and then pitching marvelously in ALCS Game 4 on three days' rest after the Yanks' first loss of the postseason.

Now the Yankees are going to have to find another way to navigate this postseason. For the first time in the playoffs, they trail in a series. Sabathia pitched tough, surviving without his best stuff. But he couldn't master Chase Utley and couldn't outpitch Cliff Lee, so now things are certainly ug-lee for the Yanks.

Lee humbled the Yankees as badly as Josh Beckett did in the last World Series game the Yankees had played before last night, Game 6 in 2003. And like Beckett in that Fall Classic, the Yankees suddenly have to worry more about what Lee might do to them on three days' rest than the implications of pitching their own big three—Sabathia, Burnett and Pettitte—short.

Lee worked quickly, pinpointed to both sides of the plate and had his full repertoire of cutter, sinker, changeup and curve peaking as he defused the usually strong weapon of Yankee patience. Forget about walks; Lee had just four three-ball counts all game.

Lee induced one feeble at-bat after another in 122 pitches of mastery. He all but had disdain in catching a Johnny Damon pop dismissively in the sixth inning and then was Globetrotteresque in grabbing a Robinson Cano grounder in the eighth with a behind-the-back snag.

The Yanks managed six hits in all—three by Derek Jeter—and there was no late-game magic this time from Alex Rodriguez, who was 0-for-4 with three strikeouts. The magic belonged to Lee, who gave up one unearned run in a 6–1 triumph that inflicted the first home loss of these playoffs on the Yankees.

The Phillies are now 3–1 in The Bronx this year, and the Yanks now need Burnett to outpitch Pedro Martinez tonight or risk heading to Philadelphia down two games to none. The Yanks could soon learn what the Mets already know: It is not easy to beat out the Phillies. These are not the Twins or Angels. These are the tough-minded defending champs.

"Don't overthink things," A-Rod said. "It was a dominant pitcher that dominated our lineup and probably would have dominated any lineup."

But it is not that simple. The Phillies also showed they can out-patient the Yankees as hitters while the Yankee set-up crew—specifically fallen wunderkind Phil Hughes—suddenly looks atrocious.

However, the big issue right now is that when it comes to aces, Sabathia is pitching terrific while Lee is pitching historic. The Phillies' lefty former-Indian Cy Young winner is going better than the Yankees' lefty former-Indian Cy Young winner. And we may see that matchup two more times.

"We are hoping he is not this good next time, but we know better," Damon said. "Our guys are going to have to shut them down, and we are going to have to win a 1–0 or 2–1 game. He is not giving up too many."

Lee has not yielded an earned run in either of his last two starts, eight innings against Joe Torre's Dodgers and now nine innings against Girardi's Yankees. He has a 0.54 ERA in four postseason starts. Before last night, he had faced the Yankees nine previous times and never struck out more than seven. He had seven in four innings in Game 1, 10 overall.

As for Sabathia, he was not particularly sharp but figured out a way to survive seven innings and permit just two runs. He never did figure out Utley, though. Sabathia had not surrendered a homer to a lefty all year at home, and then Utley went deep in both the third and sixth innings.

That was going to be enough to beat the Yankees last night. Because Lee was Grover Cleveland Alexander, Steve Carlton and the 2008 Cole Hamels rolled into one. In other words, he was as good as anyone Philadelphia has ever thrown in the postseason.

So now Girardi has to ponder how to maneuver against someone pitching this historical-Lee. ∎

The recipe for success had started with CC Sabathia winning the first game of each series to put the Yankees in the driver's seat. But after World Series Game 1, Joe Girardi had to come up with a new way to use his pitchers to maximize the probability of victory.

A.J. bests Pedro to even series

October 29, 2009 • By George A. King III

A.J. Burnett and Mariano Rivera altered the mood in the Yankees' universe last night better than any drug could have.

Armed with a filthy curveball he was able to throw for strikes, Burnett earned his October pinstripes by allowing the Phillies a run and four hits across seven innings, and Rivera supplied two shutout innings of relief as the Yankees evened the World Series with a 3–1 Game 2 victory before a Yankee Stadium crowd of 50,181.

With the best-of-seven Series tied 1–1, Game 3 is tomorrow night in Philadelphia, where Andy Pettitte opposes Cole Hamels, last year's World Series MVP the Phillies were wary of pitching in The Bronx.

Instead they went with longtime Yankees villain Pedro Martinez, who allowed three runs and six hits in six-plus innings despite not feeling very well.

"It means a lot," Burnett said of his gem. "After (Game 1) I wanted to set the tone early and be aggressive."

Signed to a five-year, $82.5-million deal to play second fiddle to CC Sabathia in the Yankees' revamped rotation, Burnett pitched like an ace.

The lone run was tainted because Alex Rodriguez failed to make a play on Matt Stairs' two-out grounder in the second inning that scored Raul Ibanez, who had reached on a double that hit right along the foul line.

Mark Teixeira halted a long slump with a solo homer in the fourth off Martinez that tied the score 1–1. Hideki Matsui, who was 30 minutes late for batting practice because of thick traffic, according to Joe Girardi, put the hosts ahead 2–1 in the sixth with a homer to right on a 74-mph curveball at 1–2.

"He threw two curveballs, and the second one was a little inside, and I made the adjustment," Matsui said. "Fortunately, it ended in a good result."

Rivera allowed two runners to reach in the eighth with one out and then fed Game 1 hero Chase Utley a 4-6-3 double-play ball, though replays showed Utley may have been safe. Rivera recorded the final three outs to hike his postseason record save total to 38.

"I had an idea tonight that definitely I would have a chance to be there for two innings," said Rivera, whose last outing was Sunday in the ALCS clincher against the Angels when he also worked two innings.

Jerry Hairston Jr., who started for an ice-cold Nick Swisher in right, led off the seventh with a single, and pinch runner Brett Gardner was running when Melky Cabrera laced a single to right.

With runners at the corners, no outs and the Yankees leading by a run, Girardi used Jorge Posada as the hitter for Jose Molina. Phils manager Charlie Manuel ignored Posada's .183 (11-for-60) career average against Martinez (including 33 strikeouts) and summoned right-hander Chan Ho Park.

Posada's single to center scored Gardner for a 3–1 lead, but the Yankees failed to pad the cushion. Curiously, Derek Jeter was bunting on three pitches—all strikes—and was out when he fouled off the third.

"I had (the bunt sign) on the first pitch, but I am not sure after that," Jeter said. "With two strikes, I shouldn't have done that."

Lefty Scott Eyre entered to face Johnny Damon, and his liner landed in Ryan Howard's glove—or at least that's what the umpires ruled even though he appeared to trap it—to start an inning-ending double play.

The Yankees have scored four runs (three earned) in two games and yet are even with three tilts slated for Philly, where Matsui will be tethered to the bench because the DH won't be in play.

"Winning tonight is very important; we didn't want to go down two games going to Philadelphia," Matsui said. "It only adds to the confidence we have."

Last night the confidence started with Burnett and ended with Rivera. ∎

A.J. Burnett pitched like an ace in Game 2, allowing the Phillies just one hard-earned run. The offense rode the long ball to chase Pedro Martinez, sending him to the dugout amidst a cacophony of sound from the fans at Yankee Stadium.

No punch: Yanks, A-Rod must step it up

October 29, 2009 • By Joel Sherman

Alex Rodriguez was so mesmerizing in the first two rounds of the playoffs that he distracted attention away from just how unimpressive the rest of the Yankees lineup was.

He hit so forcefully and dramatically that it was possible to believe the rest of the lineup could play chorus to his genius. He was breaking out, so who cared if just about everyone else was breaking down?

But what the World Series is revealing is that the chorus better be ready to do more than stand in the background. Rodriguez has turned back the clock to his previous Yankees Octobers during the first two games of the Fall Classic. He has plummeted from standout to struck out. Philadelphia pitchers have not worked around him, and Rodriguez suddenly looks as if he gobbled down a heaping helping of kryptonite.

Fortunately for the Yankees, the two players who surrounded Rodriguez in the lineup last night stirred. Mark Teixeira and Hideki Matsui each hit a solo homer off another player who temporarily turned back the clock in World Series Game 2, Pedro Martinez. Teixeira tied the score, Matsui gave the Yankees the lead, and the World Series is tied at one game apiece despite Rodriguez being hitless in eight at-bats with six strikeouts.

"I am going to bet that Alex is going to be fine the rest of the Series," Teixeira said after the Yankees beat the Phillies 3–1. "If not, me and the other guys will have to pick it up."

The first two games of this World Series touted for its powerhouse offenses has been dominated instead by three former Cy Young winners (Cliff Lee, CC Sabathia and Pedro) and Burnett at what A-Rod termed "as good as he has been all year." Burnett outdueled Martinez, holding the Phillies to one run in seven innings when allowing more could have left the Yankees desperately behind in this Series.

For right now the Yankees offense is tepid and probably about to get worse when the DH (probably Matsui) is removed from the lineup for the three games in Philadelphia. Manager Joe Girardi hinted at playing Matsui some in left, but he is unlikely to start.

Girardi did enact one bold move, removing the struggling Nick Swisher and starting Jerry Hairston in Game 2. He shunned lefties Brett Gardner and Eric Hinske because Hairston was 10-for-27 lifetime against Martinez, though his last at-bat against Pedro was in July 2004, or five years and five mph ago.

"He may not throw 98 anymore, but his command was as great as ever," Hairston said.

The Yankees led just 2–1 when Hairston led off the seventh with the first of three consecutive singles. The second, by Melky Cabrera, knocked out Martinez. The third, by pinch-hitter Jorge Posada, made it 3–1. There was still first and second and no outs. And then Girardi ordered a foolhardy sacrifice considering the next batter was Johnny Damon, who had terrible swings to that point, and lefty Scott Eyre was warmed to face him. Jeter failed twice, and then with the sacrifice off, he tried a third time anyway, bunted foul and struck out, which helped derail the Yankees from scoring further.

"That was me; that was stupid," Jeter said.

The failed sacrifice was part of a postseason-long problem for the Yankees: they have been ill with runners in scoring position (.213) and men on base (.244). Either that will have to get better, A-Rod will have to get better or both for the Yankees to beat the Phillies.

Rodriguez claims he's fine, says he took some of his best swings yesterday and just fouled pitches back that he should have hammered. The results, though, are like ghosts of horrid postseasons past. He already has one more strikeout in these two games (6) than he did in 31 at-bats over the previous two series. He went from carrying an offense to needing some best supporting actors to shine.

Teixeira, as the third-place hitter, is the most obvious candidate. He came into Game 2 hitting .186 for the postseason and was growing prickly, dismissive and evasive under questions about his October struggles. It did not fit his image as smiling and robotic. Matsui was hitting just .242 during the postseason, interspersing a few good at-bats around swaths of helpless-looking hacks.

Perhaps their homers will loosen them up and be a springboard for a Robinson Cano or Damon to start delivering more hits of meaning, too.

"I am 0-for-the-Series, and the guys picked me up today, and that makes me feel good going into Game 3," A-Rod said.

The Yankees are now facing a best-of-five series with Philadelphia owning the home-field edge. To win now, the Yankees need A-Rod to reawaken or the chorus to soar. ∎

After dominating opposing pitchers in the first two rounds of the playoffs, Alex Rodriguez's slump in the opening games of the World Series appeared to expose gaps in the Yankees offense.

Swisher & Co. provide pop for Andy

October 31, 2009 • By George A. King III

Andy Pettitte grunted through six innings without his best stuff. Nick Swisher finally broke through. Alex Rodriguez's first World Series hit was a clutch homer that needed a second look. And Joba Chamberlain and Damaso Marte took the load off Mariano Rivera.

All of that added up to an 8–5 Game 3 victory for the Yankees over the Phillies last night in front of 46,061 at Citizens Bank Park that put the Yankees in position to grab control of the Series tonight in Game 4.

The victory gave the Yankees a 2–1 lead in the best-of-seven Series. The start of the game was delayed 80 minutes by rain.

Because Joe Girardi is using ace CC Sabathia on three days' rest tonight against Joe Blanton, the Yankees are in position to cop a 3–1 lead.

Pettitte put the Yankees in a 3–0 ditch in the second when he gave up the first of Jayson Werth's two homers, issued two walks and failed to communicate with Jorge Posada on Cole Hamels' sacrifice bunt that turned into a hit.

"It was a battle tonight; I wasn't able to get the breaking ball over," said Pettitte, who allowed one hit to the final 17 batters he faced. "It was a grind tonight. I can't remember winning a (postseason) game when I struggled like I did tonight."

Pettitte—who now has 17 postseason wins, adding to his record—went six innings, gave up four runs and five hits and received support from Swisher, Rodriguez and Hideki Matsui, who all homered, and Johnny Damon, who added a two-run double. Pettitte helped himself with an RBI single off Hamels that tied the game, after Swisher snapped out of his funk with a double and fueled a three-run fifth that saw the Yankees erase a 3–2 deficit.

Rodriguez, who was 0-for-8 with six strikeouts in the first two games, hit a two-run homer to right in the fourth off Hamels that originally was ruled a double. After four of the six umpires went to the video, it was ruled a homer, and the Yankees trailed, 3–2.

"I think it was a big hit," Rodriguez said of the homer that hit a television camera near the right-field foul pole and was the Yankees' first hit. "I think it woke our offense up a little bit. It felt really good."

Damon's two-run double made it 5–3 in the fifth. Swisher homered with the bases empty in the sixth, Posada had an RBI single in the seventh and Matsui delivered a pinch-hit home run in the eighth.

After Pettitte left, Chamberlain and Marte retired six straight in the seventh and eighth. Armed with a four-run lead in the ninth, Joe Girardi brought in Phil Hughes instead of Mariano Rivera. Hughes retired the first batter, but when Carlos Ruiz homered, Girardi called for Rivera, who recorded the final two outs.

According to Phillies manager Charlie Manuel, Pettitte was able to bounce back from a shaky beginning because he handled Chase Utley, Ryan Howard and Raul Ibanez, who went a combined 0-for-9 against Pettitte and fanned six times.

"The biggest thing for Pettitte was he closed off our left-handed hitters," Manuel said. "He got our left-handed hitters out."

Hamels didn't allow a hit through three innings but appeared to let a 3–2, fourth-inning pitch to Mark Teixeira that was called a ball bother him. Rodriguez followed with the homer, and Hamels didn't get out of the fifth.

In $4\frac{1}{3}$ innings, Hamels, last year's World Series MVP, gave up five runs and five hits.

Because Girardi is going with Sabathia tonight and Manuel is saving ace Cliff Lee for tomorrow night's Game 5, the Yankees have a big chance to grab the Series by the throat with a win after so many contributions from different people last night. ■

Nick Swisher finally broke out of his postseason slump, doubling and hitting a homer in the Game 3 win. Several role players rose to the occasion in Game 3, taking the pressure off the big names for one night.

Yanks grab momentum

October 31, 2009 • By Joel Sherman

For three innings last night, the Yankees got into the Halloween spirit by coming to Game 3 of the World Series as the Kansas City Royals.

They appeared jittery and unnerved performing in a Citizens Bank Park that was an inferno of noise. Andy Pettitte, in his record-extending 39th career playoff start, was pitching defensively without his signature cutter. Alex Rodriguez looked unglued at third, and Nick Swisher did a Bobby Abreu imitation by refusing to approach the wall on a potentially catchable ball that became a Pedro Feliz double.

Meanwhile, Cole Hamels navigated once around the Yankees lineup looking like the guy who won the World Series MVP last year.

At that moment, it would have been easier to conceive of Steve Phillips as Husband of the Year than that Pettitte would outlast and outpitch Hamels or that the seething beast in this game was the Yankees' offense. But A-Rod and Swisher journeyed from defensive malfeasance to offensive stars, and the complexion of Game 3 changed 180 degrees, perhaps taking the 105th World Series with it.

The Yankees scored in five straight innings beginning in the fourth to win 8–5. They now lead two games to one, and while CC Sabathia is going tonight on three day's rest, he is facing Joe Blanton, whose 8.18 ERA vs. the Yanks is fourth worst among active pitchers (minimum four starts).

Suddenly, the Phillies' 3-4 hitters, Chase Utley and Ryan Howard, are liabilities, and from the looks of last night, Joba Chamberlain and Damaso Marte may be late-game assets.

How quickly impressions change. Just look at how stunning the transformation was in this game.

And perhaps Game 3 pivoted on mechanical and emotional adjustments made by Pettitte and Swisher.

Pettitte was on the brink of being ousted in the second. Jayson Werth led off with the first of two mammoth homers in this game. Before the inning was over, Pettitte would walk Jimmy Rollins with the bases loaded and allow a Shane Victorino sac fly. It was 3–0, and a party was underway in Philly.

Pettitte was rushing his delivery, causing his arm to drag, which robbed the bite of his cutter. This made him jumpy temperamentally, as well, at a time when one more hit might have finished him off. But in these hostile environments, Pettitte was able to recalibrate, slowing his motion. "Veteran-type guys can block stuff out and self-correct," GM Brian Cashman said. "They can take a punch in the first round and stick around for a long time."

Pettitte struck out Utley to end the third and did not allow another hit until Werth homered to open the sixth. Pettitte made it through six innings to secure perhaps the most gratifying of his record 17 postseason wins. Because he survived the hostility without his best stuff, and he preserved the bullpen with the Yanks planning to go short with their starters the rest of the way.

"He was a bulldog for us," Swisher said.

And while Swisher did not match Werth, he suddenly had worth. He was benched for Game 2 due to a horrible playoff-long slump. At that time, Girardi spoke to Swisher about the need to stop pressing and try to enjoy what could be a once-in-a-lifetime experience. And hitting coach Kevin Long convinced Swisher to spread out and use "a completely different stance" at the plate. The idea was to give Swisher more time to decipher the buffet of off-speed stuff he has seen in the postseason.

It worked. Swisher opened the fifth with a double and scored on a Pettitte single, which gave Pettitte as many hits and one more RBI than Howard has in this Series. Swisher homered in the following inning. Hamels, who did not give up a hit until A-Rod clocked a two-run, replay-aided homer in the fourth, never made it out of the fifth. Six of the final 10 batters he faced reached safely before J.A. Happ relieved, and Swisher homered off of Happ in the sixth.

"(Swisher) made a dramatic change, and it worked," Long said.

And this whole game and series has made a dramatic change now. A-Rod went from 0-for-8 with six strikeouts to having a right-field camera turn into this year's Jeffrey Maier, a ball smashing into it and becoming a homer after a replay challenge. Chamberlain and Marte went six up, six down, and the Yanks just might have the bridge they were previously lacking to Mariano Rivera.

The first pitch in Game 3 had been delayed by rain for 1 hour, 20 minutes, and then it took the Yanks an additional hour to stop being the Royals. When that happened, Game 3 and possibly the whole Series shifted toward the Yankees. ∎

With a pointed effort, Joba Chamberlain and the rest of his Yankees teammates turned the tide in Game 3—the first game of the series in Philadelphia.

A-Rod puts Yanks a win away

November 1, 2009 • By George A. King III

The Yankees are nine innings away from returning to the only place not considered a season-ending failure by Derek Jeter and others.

Tonight at Citizens Bank Park, the Yankees will attempt to win their 27th World Series title—and first since 2000—against the defending-champion Phillies.

It's all possible because of a two-out, three-run ninth-inning rally highlighted by Alex Rodriguez's go-ahead double that lifted the Yankees to a pulsating 7–4 win in Game 4, providing them a 3–1 lead in the best-of-seven Series.

"There is no question that I have never had a bigger hit," said Rodriguez. "If you look at what Mark Teixeira and I have done in this World Series, it's not much. It just tells you what a balanced team we have, and we are getting contributions from all our guys."

With the score tied 4–4, after Pedro Feliz turned a 95-mph fastball from Joba Chamberlain into a solo homer in the eighth inning, the Yankees appeared flat in the ninth against Phils closer Brad Lidge.

But a nine pitch at-bat by Johnny Damon resulted in a two-out single. With the Phillies using third baseman Feliz on the right side of second for the shift against Teixeira, Damon swiped second on the first pitch to Teixeira as Feliz took the throw at second.

Knowing that third base wouldn't be covered and believing he was faster than Feliz, Damon raced for the bag and beat Feliz there. Lidge hit Teixeira with a 1–1 pitch and gave up an RBI double to Rodriguez, who was hit in the first inning by Joe Blanton, which drew a warning to both teams because Rodriguez was drilled twice in Game 3. Jorge Posada followed with a two-run single for a three-run bulge.

Mariano Rivera, who is the favorite to win the Series MVP, recorded the final three outs for his postseason-record 39th save and second of the Series.

"I was trying to be aggressive and trying to get into scoring position," said Damon, who went 3-for-5 and scored twice. "It just worked out that there was a throw, the third baseman covered (second) and the pitcher didn't (cover third)."

Phils manager Charlie Manuel said miscommunication between Lidge and catcher Carlos Ruiz left third base naked.

A.J. Burnett, the second Yankees' hurler in two games to work on three days' rest instead of four, opposes Phillies ace Cliff Lee. If a Game 6 is required it will be played Wednesday evening at Yankee Stadium.

Working on three days' rest, CC Sabathia went 6 ⅔ innings, allowing three runs and seven hits. Prior to the game, Joe Girardi said he wouldn't use Rivera for two innings, and he stuck to the plan when Chamberlain started the eighth with a 4–3 lead.

Chamberlain fanned Jayson Werth and Raul Ibanez on 97-mph fastballs and then got ahead of Feliz, 1–2, with a pair of 96-mph fastballs. Two 87-mph sliders got the count full, and Feliz smoked a 95-mph heater into the left-field seats to tie the score, 4–4.

Sabathia was far from sharp, but he was effective when he needed to be (2-for-10 with runners in scoring position). The last hit was a two-out solo homer to Chase Utley in the seventh that cut the lead to 4–3 and forced Sabathia out of the game. ∎

A-Rod's first hit of the World Series was a bomb in Game 3 that may have turned the momentum in the favor of the Yankees for good. In Game 4, he kept the momentum rolling by doubling home a run and later scoring.

This fall, this team, is A-Rod's

November 1, 2009 • By Mike Vaccaro

It had to boil down to this, didn't it? That's always been Alex Rodriguez's rarest gift, the way the moment seeks him out, stalks him, finds him. That hasn't always been a good thing, but those moments all seem another lifetime ago. In these playoffs, there is nobody better equipped to seize them.

And nobody the Yankees would rather see stepping to home plate.

"He's the reason why we're sitting here and in Philadelphia right now," Johnny Damon would say later, after everyone could start breathing again. "Without him, who knows where our road may have stopped? He's been huge."

Damon was the reason Rodriguez was standing at home plate in the top of the ninth, with 46,145 people screaming at him, slandering him, calling him a cheat and a bum and every other standby hidden in the Philly lexicon. It was Damon who'd wrestled Brad Lidge through nine pitches of hand-to-hand combat, who'd battled from 1-and-2 down in the count to 3-and-2 to a clean single to left.

It was Damon who'd stolen second base with Mark Teixeira up, who'd made one of the greatest heads-up plays of all time by dashing to third when the Phillies left the base uncovered, who'd no doubt rattled Lidge to the point where the Phillies' closer promptly plunked Teixeira, sending him to first and all but inviting Rodriguez to the plate.

And to this moment.

Lidge, in many ways, might know more than anyone else in baseball about the demons that have plagued Rodriguez, for there have been few who've had to conquer larger ghosts.

Back in 2005, he'd famously surrendered a knee-buckling home run to Albert Pujols with his Houston Astros one out away from the World Series. From that personal piece of hell, he'd risen to go 48-for-48 in save opportunities last year and was on the mound when the Phillies won the Series.

He knows the redemptive power of autumn as well as anyone.

Now he threw a get-me-over fastball, and Rodriguez watched it zip by. The two men had faced each other only three times earlier, and A-Rod knew he'd done well: two hits, three RBIs. Back in May, he'd drilled a home run at Yankee Stadium off a Lidge fastball. He figured he'd have to get another; no way Lidge could risk burying a slider.

Lidge threw a fastball.

"I think it was a decent pitch," Lidge said.

But if you've seen Rodriguez across these playoffs, you knew it was going to take more than decent. It might have required more than Mathewson, Gibson and Maddux, to be honest, because you could almost see what was happening half a breath before it happened. His swing has been that true, his confidence that high, his performance that extraordinary. The ball leaped off his bat, and it immediately started curling away from Raul Ibanez in left, soaring beyond him.

And it was like someone kicked a plug out of the wall at Citizens Bank Park. All you could hear was the sound of Yankees screaming from the dugout, of Teixeira shouting at A-Rod from third base, of the couple thousand Yankees fans in attendance yelling themselves into a hoarse hysteria. It was 5–4, Yanks, on the way to 7–4, Yanks.

"You've got to give him credit," Lidge said. "It could have been off the plate."

It could have been six feet over his head or an inch off the ground, the way he's going. Rodriguez has preached about "swinging at strikes" all postseason, but he is in the kind of groove all players dream about and few actually attain.

He's been there an awful lot in his career, an awful lot during 15 of the greatest regular seasons anyone has ever strung together. Just never in the playoffs. Certainly never like this.

He would try to brush that aside, talking about how his struggles early in the Series, and Teixeira's throughout the playoffs, show how balanced the Yankees are.

And they are.

But A-Rod is the ballast. He is the one who saved two games that had gone to the brink earlier in the postseason, and he is the one who delivered them all to the doorstep of a 27th title last night. Standing on second base, drinking in the moment, you knew exactly how he felt, because if you cheer for the Yankees, you were feeling it too.

"I've never had a bigger hit," he said.

It would be hard to imagine he'll ever have a bigger one. Only with this player, in this season, you simply can't say that for sure. There's still room. There's still time. ■

A-Rod finally put the team on his shoulders and helped carry the Yankees through the middle part of the Series.

Yanks rally but can't dig out of A.J. hole

November 2, 2009 • By George A. King III

By the time the Yankees got into the suspect Phillies bullpen late in Game 5 last night, the early ditch A.J. Burnett had driven them into was too deep to escape.

With a chance to cop their 27th World Series title, the Yankees turned to Burnett on three days' rest instead of the customary four. Using talent evaluator language, Burnett was "short."

Paired against Phillies ace and fellow Arkansas native Cliff Lee, Burnett didn't get out of the third inning, allowed six runs and four hits, walked four and hit a batter in an 8–6 loss that was witnessed by 46,178 at Citizens Bank Park.

"I let 25 guys down. I let a whole city down," Burnett said of the miserable outing that he explained wasn't a byproduct of the short rest. "It's the worst feeling in the world. We had a chance to do something special and to fail like that..."

With a 3–2 lead in the best-of-seven Series that shifts to The Bronx for Game 6 tomorrow night, the Yankees are likely to send Game 3 winner Andy Pettitte—on three days' rest—against Pedro Martinez, who lost Game 2 despite pitching well.

"Whenever they tell me to pitch, I am ready to go," said Pettitte, who didn't think short rest would bother him. "I am plenty up to it."

The Phillies took a 3–1 lead in the opening inning on the first of Chase Utley's two homers, a three-run shot. They scored three more in the third, upping the cushion to 6–1 and chasing Burnett.

That lead was too much to overcome, although the Yankees rallied, scoring three in the eighth and one in the ninth, when they had the tying run at the plate in Derek Jeter and runners at the corners with no outs.

Jeter, a serious Series MVP candidate thanks to a .364 average, allowed the Phillies to breathe by hitting a Ryan Madson pitch on the ground to Jimmy Rollins, who started a 6-4-3 double play, though Jorge Posada scored from third. Madson was Phillies manager Charlie Manuel's choice to start the ninth instead of closer Brad Lidge, who lost Game 4 by allowing three runs in the ninth inning.

Posada opened the ninth last night with a double, and pinch-hitter Hideki Matsui's opposite-field single to left put runners at first and third before Madson got Jeter to hit into the twin killing.

"He made a good pitch, that's the bottom line," Jeter said of Madson's 2–1 offering.

Still, the Yankees weren't done. Johnny Damon, another MVP candidate with a .381 average thanks to a 3-for-4 night, singled to center. That brought Mark Teixeira, who had doubled in the eighth, to the plate, but he fanned for the final out.

Though Burnett's flameout hurt a lot, two homers given up by Phil Coke in the seventh certainly helped prevent the late noise from being loud enough.

Utley's second homer, leading off the seventh—his fifth of the Series, tying Reggie Jackson for the most in history—was followed by Raul Ibanez's two-out blast.

"I am pretty embarrassed at myself and the way that all went," Coke said of his second Series appearance. "But that's what (the next game) is for."

Alex Rodriguez, who was on deck when Teixeira ended the game with a walk-off whiff, was looking forward to going home.

"We know where we are going to be at," said Rodriguez, who doubled in the Yankees' first run in the first and had a two-run double in the eighth that chased Lee. "We did what we had to do, win two of three, and we are going home." ∎

Manager Joe Girardi finally took the ball from A.J. Burnett after he struggled in Game 5.

A.J.'s big chance goes awry

November 2, 2009 • By Mike Vaccaro

When it was over, the clubhouse boys were stuffing gear into bags rather than wrapping plastic over lockers. Instead of uncorking champagne, the Yankees were tossing socks and sanitary hose into big laundry bins. Bud Selig, with no presentation to make, walked briskly and bypassed the room altogether.

There was no music, no laughter, very little conversation, very little interaction at all. But over in the far corner of the room, one very penitent pitcher took all of this—all of the quiet, all of the disappointment, all of the frustration—and heaved it onto his shoulders like a thousand-pound knapsack.

"I let 25 guys down," A.J. Burnett said. "I let a whole city down."

He wasn't about to spare himself the rod, which is just as well, because the Phillies had already beaten him to it. So often these past few weeks, Burnett had spoken of dreaming precisely this dream a thousand times before: ball in his hand, champagne on ice in a back room, Commissioner's Trophy sitting in the house.

His dreams, though, had always shaken out differently than this.

He certainly would get more than six outs in those dreams, would always face more than 15 hitters, would surely allow a lot fewer than six runs in two-plus innings. If this really was a dream, it was directed by Tim Burton.

"If we would have pitched today, we probably would have won today," said manager Joe Girardi, who also was in no mood for euphemisms. "That's the bottom line. A.J. struggled today. That's something that happens in the game of baseball."

Maybe the Yankees were due. Maybe Burnett was due. In their first 13 games of the postseason, they'd received 13 starts of six innings or better from their three-man workhorse rotation. Burnett was responsible for four of those starts, including Game 2 of this World Series, when he'd allowed only four hits in seven innings and looked virtually unhittable.

He'd also been in an almost identical position in Anaheim two weeks ago, Game 5 of the American League Championship Series, a chance to close out the Angels, and he'd been dreadful early. But even at that—four runs scoring before he ever recorded an out—he'd gritted his way back, minimized the damage, bought the Yankees time enough to make an ill-fated comeback.

This time, it was three runs before an out, and then three more runs in the third, and Burnett didn't even wait for Girardi to reach the pitcher's mound, descending down the hill early, handing the ball to his manager on the go, his head down, a deafening band of abuse raining down from rejoicing Phillies fans.

Back in the dugout, he stared blankly into space. The Yankees had hopped on Cliff Lee early, tagged him for a run-scoring double by Alex Rodriguez, and it was apparent that Lee wasn't anywhere near the untouchable force of nature he'd been in Game 1. They handed that precious 1–0 lead to Burnett, asked him to entrust it.

"But I couldn't do anything right," he said. "I couldn't throw strikes. I couldn't locate. In Game 2, I felt like I could put the ball wherever I wanted it. Tonight..."

He let the thought hang in the air for a couple of seconds.

"Tonight," he said, "I embarrassed myself."

It got worse for Burnett after he repaired to the clubhouse, because his teammates threw the inevitable burst of terror into the Phillies, into the 46,178 inside Citizens Bank Park (less the couple of thousand boisterous Yankee fans in the left-field bleachers). The Phillies' lead reached 8–2 before Lee finally tired, and the assault was on.

It was 8–5 by the ninth. The Yankees had first and third, no one out, Derek Jeter at the plate, and a starting pitcher dying a hundred deaths in the clubhouse, watching it on television, sick to his stomach.

"If I pitch even a little bit like I'm capable of," Burnett said, "we have a real chance to win this game. A great chance. And maybe we're already celebrating in here."

But he didn't. The hole was too great. Jeter bounced into a double play, making the score 8–6 but restoring the color to 44,000 or so cheeks. Mark Teixeira struck out as the tying run. We get two more days of baseball season, at least. We get another Pedropalooza in The Bronx. All of that is fun. None of it is what A.J. Burnett had in mind.

Someone asked if he would be available to work a hitter here, an inning there in either Game 6 or, if necessary, 7. Burnett only threw 53 pitches, after all. And for the first time in a couple of hours, he started to perk up again.

"Oh, man," he said, "I would love that." ■

Despite his struggles in Game 5, Burnett was a key cog in the Yankees 2009 World Series pitching rotation.

Yankees are back where they belong

November 4, 2009 • By George A. King III

Baseball's penthouse is again decorated with handpainted silk Yankees pinstripe wallpaper. Nine years after their last World Series title, the Yankees earned No. 27 when they spanked the defending champion Phillies 7–3 in Game 6 at Yankee Stadium before a record crowd of 50,315 that didn't include George Steinbrenner.

Thursday morning the Yankees celebrated with a ticker-tape parade up lower Broadway.

"Right where we belong," Derek Jeter bellowed from a stage in the middle of the $1.5 billion Stadium.

And they looked very comfortable. Alex Rodriguez, who doesn't have to answer any more questions about choking in the postseason, let loose with a river of victory tears and promised the parade will be a huge party.

Mariano Rivera held a copy of *The Post*'s front page with the No. 27 on the cover.

Hideki Matsui, who went 3-for-4 with a homer and six RBIs that tied the single-game Series record, was named the MVP and took the occasion to lobby for a return.

"I hope so," when asked if he would be back. Matsui can become a free agent in 15 days. "I hope it works out. I love New York and I love the fans."

From 1996 to 2000 the Yankees won four Series titles and three straight (1998–2000). They came within two outs of winning in 2001, were bounced from the 2003 Series in six games and didn't make it back until this year when they spent almost a half-billion dollars of Steinbrenner's fortune to import CC Sabathia, A.J. Burnett and Mark Teixeira to successfully plug gaping holes in the rotation and lineup.

When the subject of money surfaced, general manager Brian Cashman was ready with an answer.

"You can call us anything you want. You're also going to have to call us world champions," said Cashman, who didn't join the Steinbrenner family on the stage to accept the World Series trophy.

Sabathia, Burnett and Teixeira played big roles in the Yankees' success, but it was Matsui who turned Game 6 into a knockout audition for 2009 employment.

"Tonight he was as locked in as I have ever seen him," Jeter said.

Matsui, the 2000 MVP of the Japan Series, hit a two-run homer in the second, a two-run single in the third and a two-run double in the fifth that broke the Phillies' will.

Andy Pettitte, another free-agent candidate who has a better chance of the Yankees wanting him back than Matsui, provided 5 $^2/_3$ gutsy innings on three days' rest.

Pettitte, who is 18–9 in the postseason and 4–0 this year, split to a standing ovation. He allowed three runs, four hits and five walks and became the second pitcher, following Derek Lowe in 2004, to win all three of a team's postseason series clinchers.

With copies of yesterday's *Post* poster of Pedro Martinez in a diaper being flashed around the Stadium that was filled with "Whose Your Daddy" chants, Martinez lasted only four innings. He gave up four runs and three hits, including Matsui's two-run homer.

The victory vindicated Girardi's decision to use Sabathia, Burnett and Pettitte on three days' rest instead of trusting a World Series start to Chad Gaudin. And it erased all that criticism for using so many relievers in the ALCS against the Angels.

Jeter, Rivera, Pettitte and Posada will be fitted for their fifth World Series rings, all as Yankees.

Damaso Marte topped off a wonderful Series (five Ks in 2 $^2/_3$ innings) by fanning Utley with two outs to end the seventh and Howard starting the eighth.

Girardi then called for Rivera to get the last five outs.

"I told them it was an honor to be part of their fifth championship," said Teixeira, who added an RBI single in the fifth. ∎

Jorge Posada and Derek Jeter celebrate with the World Series trophy.

Matsui brings Yanks' elusive 27th title

November 4, 2009 • By Joel Sherman

Think of the procession and the price. Think of all the stars brought in for nearly a decade at a staggering cost to try to recreate the dynasty years.

It has been quite a parade, and yet no parade.

There were Mike Mussina and Jason Giambi, Randy Johnson and Kevin Brown, Javier Vazquez and Gary Sheffield, Carl Pavano and Jeff Weaver.

They were imported for one reason, and one reason only: To bring championship No. 27 to the Bronx. And they all left ring-less.

Hideki Matsui, however, persevered through damaged knees and the loss of his regular outfield gig. He came in with a big nickname and was never more Godzilla than on possibly his last day in a Yankee uniform. The one-time Yomiuri Giant is now a giant Yankee.

Matsui went all Reggie on a Game 6 of the World Series. He was Pedro Martinez's Daddy and the MVP of the Fall Classic. He drove in a World Series–tying record six runs and pushed himself and his team to the Canyon of Heroes as the Yankees beat the Phillies 7–3.

There will be a parade this time.

"We scored seven and he drove in six," manager Joe Girardi said on the outskirts of euphoria in the clubhouse. "He carried us in Game 6."

In six games, the Yankees earned their 27th title, matching the number Girardi boldly wore on his back after succeeding Joe Torre. Derek Jeter, Andy Pettitte, Jorge Posada and Mariano Rivera all got one for the thumb. Alex Rodriguez, like Matsui a big-money import who had traveled long to this moment, shucked his choke label and won a legacy-burnishing championship.

Mark Teixeira, CC Sabathia and A.J. Burnett avoided the long ride of Matsui and A-Rod by winning in their first season as huge investments. And general manager Brian Cashman, who under a barrage of criticism re-signed last year saying he wanted to change his story, did that by bringing in pieces big and small that unified into a force.

But on the final day of a season that will be remembered for pies in the face and homers in the seats, Matsui did the most to assure there was no winner-take-all Game 7 today with Sabathia on short rest.

As Matsui hoisted the MVP trophy overhead from a makeshift stage in center field, Yankees assistant general manager Jean Afterman watched from near the pitcher's mound with tears in her eyes. She had once been Hideki Irabu's representative and her expertise in Japan was part of her appeal to the Yankees.

"This is why he made the journey here," Afterman said. "His favorite player of all-time is Babe Ruth, and he played 10 years in Japan [to gain free agency] to come here and be a Yankee; for this moment."

Before last night, the closest Matsui had come to a championship was his first season. He doubled as part of the eighth-inning uprising that tied ALCS Game 7 when Red Sox manager Grady Little left Pedro Martinez out on the mound on fumes. The Yankees went to the World Series on Aaron Boone's 11th-inning homer, lost to Florida and never returned. Until this year, and there was Martinez in front of Matsui yet again.

In the second inning, Martinez pitched carefully to A-Rod, walking him on four pitches. But the land mine was Matsui. Pedro had no weapons to get him out, and at the end of an eight-pitch duel he left an 87-mph fastball over the plate. Matsui took it to the second deck. It was his third homer in this Series, though he did not start three DH-less games in Philadelphia.

Showing a Little mind, Phillies manager Charlie Manuel left Martinez in to face Matsui with the bases full in the third, two outs and lefty J.A. Happ warmed, though Matsui had eight hits in his previous 18 postseason at-bats off Martinez, six for extra bases. Matsui lined a two-run single. He added a two-run double off Happ in the fifth. The score was 6–1, and the MVP of the 2000 Japan Series accepted a standing ovation back to the dugout.

In his first-ever game at Yankee Stadium, Matsui hit a grand slam. Still the gigantic homer hitter of Tokyo never materialized. Matsui's time with the Yankees, instead, has been defined by clutch at-bats and humility belying his overwhelming stardom back home. Now Matsui faces free agency and with those dubious knees and advancing age he might not be back.

"It's been a long road and a very difficult journey," Matsui said. "But I am just happy that after all these years we were able to win and reach the goal I had come here for."

If this is the pinstriped end for Matsui, then it concluded perfectly: He will be Godzilla in the Canyon of Heroes. ■

Hideki Matsui smashed and bashed his way to six RBIs and won the World Series MVP.

Larger than life on the field, CC Sabathia considers himself a pretty laid-back guy when he's away from the ballpark.

Q&A

The Post's Steve Serby chatted with the Yankees' ace lefty who is beginning his seven-year, $161-million contract.

CC Sabathia

Q: What did you weigh at birth?

A: Eight pounds, six ounces.

Q: Heaviest you've ever been?

A: 315.

Q: Weight now?

A: 309.

Q: What is your playing weight?

A: Anywhere from 300 to 305.

Q: Jersey size?

A: 56.

Q: Waist?

A: 44.

Q: Do you have a special diet?

A: I watch what I eat. My wife is a pretty good cook.

Q: Favorite item at Tao?

A: Kobe beef.

Q: Your mound temperament?

A: I like to think it's pretty even-keeled. I'm usually a pretty laid-back guy. Once I get on the mound, I get a little revved up. I try to keep my emotions under wraps…having fun.

Q: Tell me about a time when you couldn't keep your emotions in check.

A: Ohmigod! Since I've been able to do that, I've been a better pitcher. All the way up to 2004, 2005, I'd get a bad call— I'd think a ball is a strike, and they call it a ball—I'd get upset.

Q: Your most emotional moment?

A: It had to be 2004 in Chicago. I threw a curveball to Jose Valentin, and I thought it was a strike; he called it a ball. I threw my arms up, cussing…the umpire came from behind the plate. It was a big ordeal.

Q: You didn't get thrown out?

A: I was close, though.

Q: You know LeBron (James)?

A: I got a chance to watch him when he was in high school.

Q: Knicks fans want to know if you'll help them recruit LeBron.

A: I'll do my best (chuckles).

Q: What kind of guy is he?

A: He's a great dude, especially for as big a superstar as he is.…He's real humble.

Q: Do you think LeBron would be a good fit for New York?

A: I do, I really do. The biggest city in the world…the biggest stage. It would be the perfect place for him.

Q: Three dinner guests?

A: (President Barack) Obama, Jackie Robinson, Michael Jordan.

Q: Why Jackie Robinson?

A: Just to talk to him about what he went through.

Q: Why Obama?

A: Just to congratulate him and tell him what an inspiration he is.

Q: Why Jordan?

A: He's the ultimate competitor, man. Just to talk to him about what he thought in big-game situations.

Q: He had that killer instinct.

A: Exactly.

Q: Do you?

A: I like to think that I have that.

Q: You're driven to win a World Series?

A: Yeah. That's why I'm here.

Sabathia admires the killer instinct in the great competitors of sport, an attribute he hopes that he brings to the mound every time he pitches.

Well aware that staying within himself is the key to postseason success, Sabathia has brought his usual even-keel to the Yankees, from Opening Day to the World Series.

Q: What have you learned about pitching in the postseason?

A: Just do my job and not try to do too much. I felt like I had to throw eight innings of shutout ball.

Q: Your first All-Star Game in 2003?

A: I was just kinda in awe. I didn't get a chance to play, which was good.

Q: Get any autographs?

A: I'm really an autograph hound, man.

Q: What autographs did you get?

A: I got A-Rod; I got Barry (Bonds); I got a Hank Blalock; I got Magglio (Ordonez).

Q: Never got (Derek) Jeter?

A: I got his jersey a couple of years ago. I go to our equipment manager and order different guys' jerseys and then I'll get (them) signed.

Q: The dwindling number of African American baseball players concerns you?

A: Baseball's a sport where you go out and play catch with your dad. There are not a lot of fathers in a lot of African American communities; there are a lot of single parents....Kids grow up with their grandmothers and grandfathers....The easiest thing to do is grab a basketball or throw a football in the street.

Q: First tattoo?

A: Double C up on my shoulder.

Q: Favorite tattoo?

A: I've got my (three) kids' footprints from when they were born (on my forearm).

Q: Why do you wear your hat cocked?

A: It feels straight to me when I have it on.

Q: The time your mother (Margie) sent you home during a game when you were 10?

A: I had given up a home run. I was the first hitter up, and I struck out. I threw my bat and started crying. She went like this (come here motion). I knew exactly what she meant. She told me to go home. I hopped on my bike and packed up my stuff. She was all about sportsmanship and things.

Q: What did she tell you when she got home?

A: She was yelling. She was pretty upset. If I ever did anything like that, she'd take me completely out of sports.

Q: Getting robbed at gunpoint seven years ago?

A: I put myself in a bad situation. Wrong place, wrong time.

Q: Was it scary?

A: It was definitely scary having a gun pointed in your face and you're laying on the ground (with) my cousin sitting right next to me.

Q: Pitchers you liked watching?

A: Tom Glavine when I was young…A.J. (Burnett)… Randy Johnson.

Q: Starting your sixth Opening Day…as a Yankee?

A: If I am the guy, I'll definitely be honored to be able to start for this organization—especially with the pitching staff we have.

Q: Boyhood idol?

A: Ken Griffey Jr. I was a left-handed hitter.

Q: UCLA recruited you out of high school as a tight end?

A: UCLA wanted me to play just football only. Cal wanted me to play football only. A couple of schools wanted me to play basketball only.

Q: Favorite tight end?

A: Keith Jackson.

Q: You played power forward in high school?

A: I averaged 10 rebounds. I was that guy who did all the dirty work.

Q: You've met John Cena?

A: My son loves him, We watch wrestling all the time.

Q: Your son Carsten Charles III is a huge baseball fan?

A: He kept saying, "When are you playing for the Yankees?" He wanted me to play for the Yankees so bad.

Q: Why?

A: He plays Power Pros on Wii. The Yankees are his favorite team on that game.

Q: His favorite Yankee?

A: Derek Jeter, of course.

Q: Does your son remind you of you growing up?

A: Everybody says I was like that. My dad used to tell me I'd watch Raider games with him.

Q: It's tough being a Raiders fan right now?

A: It is, right now, but hopefully they'll turn it around. They got JaMarcus (Russell)….Maybe they'll draft (wide receiver Michael) Crabtree and see how it goes.

Q: The Seahawks will grab him (at No. 4; the Raiders pick seventh).

A: I like (Missouri wide receiver Jeremy) Maclin though.

Q: Your one-hitter (Aug. 31, 2008, at Pittsburgh) some thought should have been a no-hitter.

A: I thought it was a one-hitter. If I make the play, it would have been a no-hitter, but I didn't make the play. It was my own fault. It falls on my shoulders.

Q: You had planned on having your marriage proposal videotaped on Christmas morning?

A: It was supposed to be a big production. I got nervous about what I was gonna say. I got on my knees privately up in our bedroom the night before. Everybody was upset with me.

Q: You used to have a Rottweiler named Halle?

A: We're in the process of getting a German shepherd.

Q: Favorite NYC things?

A: My wife (Amber) likes to shop. I like to shop.

Q: Favorite childhood memory?

A: Going to Disneyland with my parents when I was 7.

Q: How did your parents splitting when you were 13 affect you?

A: It really didn't. My mom did a great job never bad-mouthing my father. She always pushed for us to get closer.

Q: And you did?

A: When he came out to Cleveland and lived with me for a year and a half before he passed away.

Q: Favorite meal?

A: Thanksgiving at my aunt's house.

Q: Favorite movie?

A: *Coming to America*.

Q: Favorite actor?

A: Denzel Washington.

Q: Favorite actress?

A: Halle Berry.

Q: Favorite entertainer?

A: Jay-Z.

Q: Strikeouts For Troops?

A: Barry Zito called me up and asked me if I wanted to be part of it. I was definitely all in for that. ∎

Season recap

Stories & columns from select games in the regular season

Misty eyes gaze upon facade of glory days

April 16, 2009 • By Mike Vaccaro

The eyes tell you everything. The eyes show you the way. As it always used to be, so it is again: No matter where you are inside Yankee Stadium, upper deck or lower bowl, behind home plate or off in the wings of the mezzanine, $2,500 primo seat or 14-buck bleacher slab, eventually the eyes all fix on the same thing.

The facade. The frieze. The emblem. The unofficial logo.

"The first time I walked into the old Stadium, that took my breath away," an old Yankee pitcher named Bob Turley said before the first game the Yankees would play in their new home. "And there it is."

"That," Yogi Berra said yesterday, "brings me back."

There wasn't a lot else to do that trick yesterday, not on an afternoon when the Yankees would get squashed by the Cleveland Indians, 10–2. Not with CC Sabathia needing 122 pitches to labor through 5⅔ innings. Not with the bullpen imploding behind him. Not with the Yankees' bat rack in splinters.

Will that be okay a week from now, a month from now or, let's be honest, today? Of course not.

But yesterday wasn't about the emerging worries visible on the Yankee roster, because the Yankees had in their possession the kind of secret weapon that only they own. Most sports franchises run out of answers when today becomes too bleak. Not the Yankees—because the Yankees own more yesterdays than any team in the history of professional sports. And so they can trot out Berra to throw the first pitch in the new yard, and they can invite Bernie Williams to pick a little jazz guitar in

center field, and they can bring Paul O'Neill and Boomer Wells and Tino Martinez into a new cauldron of sound.

There have been a lot of ballparks that have opened in a lot of cities over the last 20 years; but only the Yankees can put one of Babe Ruth's old bats at home plate—the one he used to swat the first homer ever hit at the old place, across the street, 86 years ago—and then have Derek Jeter give a head fake to the bat boy, as if he wanted to take a hack with that 48-ounce beauty of a billy club. "It's a new Stadium, but I think they did a tremendous job in terms of bringing a lot of the characteristics of the old Stadium over here," Jeter said.

There is a lot to be cynical about at both of the city's new ball yards, if that's how you want to go.

Met fans have howled all week about obstructed views. Yankee fans bit down hard as they wandered the grounds in search of marked-up gastronomic delights.

But baseball isn't supposed to be for the cynics. It's supposed to be for the dreamers, even on a billion-dollar field of dreams. Even in a place where advertisements hang like wallpaper on every available inch. Even when the payroll of the current team could have built 100 versions of the original Stadium.

Maybe that's when the eyes need most to look skyward, when they most need to lock with that wonderful new frieze, which looks so much like the wonderful old frieze.

A little taste, a slight whisper, of yesterday, on the day when the Yankees officially began to leave all their yesterdays across the street. ■

Beaming as he hurled the first pitch at new Yankee Stadium, 83-year-old Yogi Berra spoke of the field with a kind of boyish wonder that he compared to seeing the original ballpark for the first time six decades ago.

Star is born as Stadium opens

April 16, 2009 • By Jeremy Olshan

Yankee fans stood in awe of their sun-soaked new Stadium yesterday as they ushered in a new era of baseball in The Bronx.

A ceaseless barrage of camera flashes began during the elaborate opening ceremony for the new Yankee Stadium and didn't let up until well after the final out.

"I took 125 pictures already, and we haven't even gotten to our seats yet," gushed Anna Garzil, 34, of Mount Vernon, N.J., one of many snapping shots of everything—even the fancy new garbage cans.

The masses arrived hours before the first pitch and seemed to care more about exploring the new ballpark—which they said had a "new-car smell"—than watching the scoreboard.

What they found was a cleaner, kinder and gentler version of the old stadium.

Even the typically hostile bleachers now have several "ambassadors" holding up signs that read, "How may I help you?"

Ambassador José Morel, 26, of The Bronx, said fans were stunned to be offered assistance.

"Mainly, they ask three questions," he said. "1. How do I get to Monument Park? 2. Do I need to pay to go to the Mohegan Sun sports bar? And 3. Can you take my picture?"

But fans blown away by the $1.5 billion ballpark were far less wowed by the product on the field—a crushing 10–2 loss to Cleveland.

"Don't worry; we'll be back," said 12-year-old Jake Glantz, who left with a smile. "This place is amazing. I love it."

The day started with Derek Jeter toting to home plate the bat Babe Ruth used to swat a home run that christened the original Yankee Stadium in 1923.

The pregame ceremony also included many of the high priests of pinstripes—including Yogi Berra, Whitey Ford and Reggie Jackson—who took the field to huge ovations.

John Fogerty played his hit "Centerfield" in center field, before former Yankee center fielder Bernie Williams played a jazzy version of "Take Me Out to the Ballgame" on guitar.

Berra stood halfway between the mound and the plate to toss out the ceremonial first pitch—a little dribbler he laughed off. Kelly Clarkson sang the national anthem as fighter jets buzzed the stadium.

The best seats sell for an unheard-of $2,625 each—but the same view can be had for a fraction of that by standing behind those fans.

"I paid $14 and have as good a view, so the joke's on them," said Albie Garcia, 24.

Others were willing to plunk down 20 times the ticket price just to get inside.

"I paid $300 for a $14 seat in the bleachers, but it was worth it just to be here," said Peter Holderlin, 60. "I just wish I could have afforded bringing my kids."

Beer once again pours freely in the bleachers, but not all are thrilled. "Nobody wants this detail now," one cop told the *Post*.

On one of the long lines to the bathrooms, one fan noted that the floors were all sparkling clean and fresh smelling.

"Don't worry; we'll dirty this place up," another fan said. ∎

The glittering new home of the Yankees is the premier park in the major leagues. Opening Day could not have gone better—except for the loss to Cleveland.

Three-run HR injects life into Yankees

May 8, 2009 • By George A. King III

He begs you to watch because he wants your attention. You train your eyes on him because no matter his many faults, he can't be ignored.

So, when Alex Rodriguez re-entered the Yankees' universe in the first inning last night at Camden Yards, nobody at the ballpark or watching at home went to the bathroom or for a beer.

Making his first appearance of the season after March 9 surgery on his right hip, Rodriguez swatted the first pitch he saw from Jeremy Guthrie for a three-run homer.

Try selling that to Hollywood.

"The most unbelievable thing I have seen," A.J. Burnett said of Rodriguez's homer, which, with CC Sabathia's complete-game effort, carried the Yankees to a much-needed, 4–0 win over the Orioles in front of 36,926.

The victory halted a season-high, five-game losing streak for the Yankees.

"It was nice to get to the ballpark, give the guys a hug and do what I do best," Rodriguez said.

Nobody in baseball does what Rodriguez does. He is the best player but also a magnet for controversy and distractions. Last night wasn't only his first game back from hip surgery. It also was his initial regular-season game since he admitted in February that he used steroids while with the Rangers. And there is more. Rodriguez hadn't taken a big-league swing since the publication of a book claiming he used steroids in high school and as a Yankee. Before the game, he denied both acts.

"When I am motivated, I know what I can do," said Rodriguez, who looked rusty in his next three at-bats, when he struck out twice and grounded out. He also admitted being a step slow in the field.

Even though he missed 28 games and said his hip will require physical therapy every day, Rodriguez wasn't going to ease into Guthrie and his above-average heater.

"I wanted to be assertive in the strike zone," said Rodriguez, who timed the 97-mph fastball perfectly and drove in Johnny Damon and Mark Teixeira, who had drawn consecutive one-out walks.

Rodriguez is never going to be the most popular player in the clubhouse. But when the ball started climbing, his teammates rushed to the top step of the third-base dugout and looked left.

"Everybody was excited," said Sabathia, who easily turned in the best effort as a Yankee. "It was unbelievable, the first pitch, and he goes deep. It pumped me up."

Considering the Yankees had gone 5-for-40 (.150) with runners in scoring position during the five-game downer, Rodriguez's homer was a colossal lift.

Although Sabathia finished with a four-hit shutout, he was in trouble in the first inning and needed to be bailed out by catcher Francisco Cervelli, who made his second big-league start.

With runners on first and second and one out, Brian Roberts stole third, and Adam Jones appeared to have second swiped. However, Cervelli's throw to Robinson Cano and Cano's quick swipe tag caught Jones. Buoyed by the play, Sabathia retired Melvin Mora on a grounder to Rodriguez.

After Jones' single, Sabathia retired 23 of the next 24 batters. The only base runner was Roberts, who drew a two-out walk in the third.

Working with a nasty cutter and a fastball that was clocked at 94 mph in the ninth, Sabathia gave up two singles to start the final frame.

With nobody throwing in the bullpen, it was Sabathia's game, and he responded by striking out Jones, Nick Markakis and Mora.

"It was one swing, and the rest was CC," Rodriguez said.

But what a swing. ■

With the Yankees struggling out of the gates, the return of Alex Rodriguez sparked the club to a big win in Baltimore. Though it was early in the season, Rodriguez's homer in his first at-bat of the year may have been a turning point for 2009.

Fantasy start for Alex's last chance

May 8, 2009 • By Joel Sherman

Alex Rodriguez explained it was time to grow up, and he said he will do that by devoting himself more than ever to the children's game called baseball. He then did something from a kid's backyard fantasy: he joined the 2009 major league season already in progress and hit a three-run home run on the first pitch he saw, with only the whole baseball world watching. It was a *Natural* moment from the Unnatural, the tainted star.

Both the Yankees and A-Rod attempted to downplay his being a savior for the struggling, tense team. But by so dramatically turning around a 97-mph Jeremy Guthrie fastball in the first inning, Rodriguez gave the Yanks their first lead and their first chance to exhale since last Saturday. Normally a transmitter of stress, Rodriguez made everyone shake their heads at him again, but this time in amazement, not dismay.

"It's impressive, but you kind of expect it," CC Sabathia said. "He's the best player in the game."

On this night, the best player finally hit cleanup in Game 29, Sabathia portrayed a four-hit-throwing ace, and all looked proper—for one day anyway—with the Yankees in a 4–0 win over Baltimore.

For Rodriguez, this was down payment on his plans to make this season like 2007, when he delivered one huge hit after another en route to his third AL MVP Award. He described that season as one in which he focused maniacally on just baseball, blocking out the distractions that essentially have defined his career. He made it all about himself and the ball, and when it is just Rodriguez and the ball, he generally has the most talent on the field. As he showed against Guthrie, A-Rod is the one who makes the kids' game look the easiest.

Now a cynic would recall that 2007 was his opt-out year, and so he ended up with 275 million reasons why obsessing on his game was worthwhile.

But let's put the cynic away for now. Against history and better judgment, let's take Rodriguez at his word. He does not do sincerity easily, and yesterday he acted and sounded as close to at peace and sincere as you will find him. This was the first day of the rest of his baseball life, and the message he came with was this: I have made a lot of mistakes on and off the field, but I have a lot of baseball and life left to do something about it.

He has about eight years and five months remaining on his contract, time to play about as many games as Thurman Munson did as a Yankee. Becoming a great player and good man would not clean up the steroids and the all the buffoonish, reckless behavior of recent years. But it is not inconsequential.

"I still believe that over the next nine years I can have a happy ending," Rodriguez said.

He said the steroid revelations, the hip injury and the general dismantling of his life forced him "to look in the mirror." Somewhere on what he called the "long road" from surgery in Colorado, to rehab in Tampa, to renewal in Baltimore, he decided to strip away the extraneous layers in his life that included him keeping the public-relations industry afloat in a bad economy. He insisted his posse for this trip was trimmed to just his longtime pal, Gui Socarras, and his brother, Joe. He nearly had the game taken away by cheating and injury and now says, "I am hungry to play baseball. I have never been hungrier."

This is the right attitude. Everything good in Rodriguez's life starts on the field: him against the baseball. So, redemption begins there. Does he have the discipline to stick to that plan? His history is not good; his words of promise not often meeting his actions.

"I have nine years to make a difference, to become a better baseball player and person," Rodriguez said.

He does not get a complete do-over; the past record is the past record. But A-Rod has another chance that not many get: The opportunity to grow up and play baseball all at once. ∎

Despite the weight of his critics and his ailing hip, Alex Rodriguez came up with a big 2009, hammering 30 homers and knocking in 100 RBIs for the 13th time in his career.

Bombers' streak hits 5 after third straight walk-off win

May 17, 2009 • By Mark Hale

The wrestling championship belt was Johnny Damon's reward. It was Melky Cabrera's on Friday and Alex Rodriguez's on Saturday. It's become a Yankees tradition.

The Yankees have developed a practice of giving the WWE replica championship belt to the player that contributes most to any win.

"We pass this along to whatever player does okay during the game or helps us win," Damon said.

The prize has gone from Cabrera to A-Rod to Damon this series, because of a remarkable weekend run in which the Yankees have won three consecutive games in walk-off fashion. On Friday, Cabrera delivered a two-run single in the ninth. On Saturday, Rodriguez slammed a two-run homer in the 11th. And yesterday Damon made it three in a row, swatting a solo homer into the second deck in right in the 10th, to lead the Yankees to a 3–2 win over the Twins at the Stadium for their fifth straight victory.

"It is amazing," manager Joe Girardi said. "I've never been a part of something like this, three in a row."

"I've never seen it in my career," Rodriguez added.

The last time the Yankees had three consecutive walkoff wins was Aug. 27–29, 1972, when the Bombers did it twice to the Royals and once to the Rangers.

The Yankees, who are 20–17, have five walk-off victories this season.

A.J. Burnett, who allowed two runs in 6⅔ innings, continued making his whipped-cream pies. Burnett nailed Cabrera and A-Rod with whipped cream in the face on Friday and Saturday and doused Damon yesterday.

Not that Damon minded. In fact, he discovered a beauty tip.

"I'll take it anytime," he said. "One thing that I did figure out is whipped cream actually makes a real good hair product."

The game started off as a pitching duel between Burnett and Minnesota's Kevin Slowey (two runs, 7⅔ innings). It was scoreless until the seventh, when the Twins took a 2–0 lead on Mike Tolbert's RBI single and Burnett's wild pitch. But the Yankees tied it in the bottom of the inning on A-Rod's leadoff homer and Cabrera's sacrifice fly.

Mark Teixeira and Twins catcher Joe Mauer then made phenomenal defensive plays to keep the game tied at 2. In the eighth, the Twins loaded the bases, and Denard Span grounded a Brett Tomko pitch toward the right side, but Teixeira made a terrific diving stop and fired home from his knees for the force out.

"It was unbelievable," Tomko said.

Mauer's play was just as impressive. In the ninth, Brett Gardner was on second with one out, and Francisco Cervelli hit a comebacker that reliever Jose Mijares blocked with his glove. Mauer grabbed the ball and faked a throw to first as the speedy Gardner was trying to score from second, setting up a race to the plate like a tailback and a linebacker both angling for the end zone.

Mauer dove, tagging Gardner to keep the Yankees from winning at that point in even more bizarre walk-off fashion.

"I guess I thought he was going to throw it to first and he didn't, and he beat me to it," Gardner said.

But an inning later, Damon won it and earned the championship belt, which rested on his left shoulder. Damon said he got the belt from Burnett's son after Damon showed him some wrestling moves, and he thinks it's been a player reward since after the first homestand.

The belt, which says "CHAMP" on it, is from the WWE.

"Best family entertainment going," Damon said. ∎

—Additional reporting by Fred Kerber

Throughout 2009, fans who came out to Yankee Stadium were virtually guaranteed to get their money's worth, often having to stick it out until the last at-bat for a dramatic Yankees win. The energetic style of the team captivated fans, and as the wins rolled up, the smiles in the clubhouse grew bigger.

Yanks rip shaky Santana to nab Series edge

June 14, 2009 • By George A. King III

With Johan Santana on the Yankee Stadium mound yesterday, the Mets had a big chance to take two of three Subway Series games from the Yankees and announce to the NL East they weren't going to succumb to injury and Luis Castillo's leaky leather.

Stunningly, it was nothing more than a puncher's chance against an opponent with bigger muscles who was ready to slug.

By the second inning, Santana was on shaky pins. And before he registered an out in the fourth, the best pitcher in the National League had vanished, and the Mets were on their way to an embarrassing 15–0 loss in front of 47,943.

"It was a bad day, actually one of the worst of my career," said Santana, who was rocked for a career-high nine runs and nine hits in three-plus innings. "There are no excuses or anything; today was just a rough day."

The win enabled the Yankees to take two of three in the first set of Subway Series games and rinse away some of the foul taste of losing three straight to the Red Sox earlier in the week.

"I am not sure, great at-bats from our guys," manager Joe Girardi said of his lineup, which produced a season- high in runs, 17 hits and broke out of an extended slump with runners in scoring position by going 9-for-20 after collecting six hits in the previous 38 (.158) at-bats.

Along with the Red Sox's 11–6 loss to the Phillies, the win also reduced Boston's AL East lead to two games. The Mets dropped four games behind the front-running Phillies in the NL East.

A.J. Burnett, who was kicked hard by the Red Sox in his previous start, was the beneficiary of the hitting orgy and improved to 5–3. He allowed four hits, four walks and fanned eight in seven innings.

The only stressful inning Burnett worked was the third, after the Yankees had copped a 4–0 lead. Burnett loaded the bases with two walks and a single without an out but fanned Alex Cora and Fernando Martinez before watching Carlos Beltran's liner find Derek Jeter's glove.

"I mixed in off-speed pitches in fastball counts," said Burnett, whose breaking stuff was filthy and augmented by a 96-mph fastball. "The Beltran at-bat was a hook and then a heater away. It was a big inning."

Jeter (4-for-4; two RBIs) led the hitting display that included two-run homers by Robinson Cano (3-for-4; three RBIs) and Hideki Matsui. Francisco Cervelli went 3-for-5 and drove in a run.

When Santana gave up four runs in the second, many figured that was it for the Yankees against the ultracompetitive lefty. A perfect third, when he retired Mark Teixeira, Alex Rodriguez and Cano, was an indication Santana was back on track.

But Nick Swisher led off the fourth with a walk, Matsui homered, Cabrera doubled, Cervelli reached on an infield single and Jeter rifled a single to left.

Jerry Manuel called "Uncle" and summoned Brian Stokes from the pen. The beating continued when Johnny Damon doubled home two runs and Teixeira reached on an infield single. Rodriguez's grounder to shortstop Cora resulted in two outs and scored Jeter. Cano followed with a two-run homer, and Cabrera doubled in Swisher and Matsui, who walked.

One day after Fernando Nieve, a 26-year-old with a short and pedestrian resume, handcuffed the Yankees, they drubbed the best pitcher in the NL.

"(Santana) pitched pretty much the same," said Matsui, who was 6-for-18 (.333) against Santana coming into the game and crushed a 2–1 fastball for his 10th homer. "He struggled with his command today. That was pretty much the difference."

And the end of the Mets' chance. ■

In the first Subway Series of the year, Johan Santana was no match for the Yankee assault, yielding nine runs over three-plus innings in his worst outing of the year. The Yankees shook off a cold stretch, snagging two of three from their rivals from Queens.

A Subway stompin'

June 14, 2009 • By Mike Vaccaro

It isn't supposed to sound this way in here, inside the House That Ruthless Built. The Bronx is the borough of baseball fellowship, where good things happen, where angst is in short supply. You want angst? Take the Triborough. Go to Queens.

That's the blueprint anyway.

The reality? At the end of a rough week, A.J. Burnett was turning the 47,943 people inside Yankee Stadium into the kind of tough crowd you find at an open-mike night. The Yankees had staked him to a 4–0 lead. They had started what would become a fearsome beating on Johan Santana.

"They tried to make my job easier," Burnett said of the offense.

Now this: a leadoff walk to Daniel Murphy. A bleeding single to Brian Schneider. A full-count walk to Luis Castillo. And, now, two balls to start off Alex Cora, the Mets' portion of the audience fully engaged now, the Yankees' segment starting to make all the fretting, ominous noises you generally find over at Citi Field when the home team is fraying nerves.

This is the kind of week it had been, after all, beginning in Boston, extending here, a week that stood at a win and four losses, a week everyone understands should have been 0–5, if not for a pop fly that will live in infamy. This is the kind of week the Yankees' pitching staff had endured, a blur of ineffectiveness, and inefficiency, of wildness and woe.

The Yankees believed they had built the kind of rotation that makes losing streaks all but impossible, and yet in five straight games, the best they could muster was the seven-plus-inning, four-run effort CC Sabathia turned in Thursday night at Fenway Park. Burnett, who began the skid by getting shelled at Fenway on Tuesday, had started this game brilliantly, six up and six down with a minimum of effort. He had gotten those four runs up on the board behind him.

Now this.

"Here's what I knew," Burnett said. "I knew I had to start making pitches. I knew that I had to find a way to minimize the damage there. And I knew that I needed to step up and figure something out. And quick."

Burnett got a borderline call from home plate umpire Jim Wolf to get back in the count, then another, then got a little more help from third-base ump Gary Cederstrom, who called Cora out on what may have been a half swing but looked more like a quarter swing. That seemed to change everything. Burnett overpowered Fernando Martinez, getting him on a curve (one of about a dozen yesterday that looked like they came fresh from the curveball textbook).

By now, Yankee Stadium had returned to sounding like Yankee Stadium, which means the fans started to expect good things again, rather than waiting for the sky to fall. And so it was with almost a whiff of inevitability that a line drive that rocketed off Carlos Beltran's bat zipped on a rope toward short and straight into Derek Jeter's glove.

End of inning. End of crisis.

And the beginning of a carnival. For a change, it was the Yankees who could watch someone else's high-priced pitcher all but call for the batting- practice shield to prevent injury. Before Santana could get an out in the fourth inning, he was gone, allowing nine runs, his ERA inflated by almost a full run thanks to one awful day at the office. Awful if you're Santana, anyway.

Beautiful if you are the Yankees, at the end of a rough week, so rough you're almost grateful for the 2–4 record, knowing it could have been a lot worse, grateful for a 15–0 whitewash as welcome as a cold beer on the Fourth of July. A week that started in first place and nearly ended with stadium workers having to build an octagon ring so Francisco Rodriguez and Brian Bruney could settle things old-school.

"It's been a pretty tough go of things," manager Joe Girardi said. "Santana is always tough on us. But he's human."

The Yankees were grateful to catch him on perhaps his most human day. And weren't about to apologize. After the week they've had? Are you kidding? ∎

In the summer months, any win can help make the difference in the September playoff hunt, so it's important to seize the opportunity. With A.J. Burnett dealing and Johan Santana reeling, the Yankees did just that.

Yanks do little Wang in Subway sweep

June 28, 2009 • By Bart Hubbuch

Mariano Rivera's historic night only added to the Replace-Mets' shame. Rivera not only became just the second player ever to record 500 saves, but the Yankees' closer also notched his first career RBI in a 4–2 win that completed a three-game Subway Series sweep at Citi Field and extended the Mets' swoon.

Mets closer Frankie Rodriguez made his team a punch line in the ninth inning when he walked Rivera on a 3–2 pitch with the bases loaded to force in a run as the remaining pro-Yankees crowd erupted in laughter and cheers.

There was plenty for the Yankees to celebrate as Rivera completed a four-out save as the last of three relievers to shut out the Mets over the final 4 2/3 innings.

"The RBI means more because it was my first, and this was my 500th save," Rivera said. "But don't get me wrong—it's definitely special. To be the second guy in the history of baseball (to get 500 saves) is special."

As for the injury-ravaged Mets, who dropped to .500 at 37–37, there was only more misery. In fact, this is how bad it's gotten: they couldn't even bang around Chien-Ming Wang.

The much-maligned right-hander came in sporting an 11.20 ERA, but manager Jerry Manuel's Mets helped Wang pick up his first win of the season and pick up where CC Sabathia and A.J. Burnett had left off the previous two nights.

Wang's season-best outing also might have been the final embarrassing push Mets general manager Omar Minaya needed to get his offense-starved team a bat.

Wang (1–6) wasn't overpowering by any means, but he allowed just two runs (a season low) in 5 1/3 innings (a season high)—in a solid, 85-pitch outing.

Then again, Wang didn't need to be overpowering against a Mets offense so anemic that Manuel finally admitted before the game that he wants Minaya to make a trade.

"We had some opportunities, but it just appears as though offensively right now, any time we flinch, we're not able to overcome them," Manuel said glumly.

The Mets' five hits last night actually marked an improvement, considering their equivalent of a Triple-A lineup had mustered just four hits combined in back-to-back losses to Sabathia and Burnett to start this leg of the crosstown rivalry.

Neither total was going to get it done, and the result was a Subway Series to forget for the Mets. The Yankees took the season series 5–1 while outscoring the Mets 33–3 over the final four meetings.

With the Mets unable to get going against Wang, the Bombers got all the cushion they needed with a three-run first inning against Livan Hernandez.

The quick deficit wasn't entirely Hernandez's fault; his problems seemed to compound after a boneheaded throwing decision by now part-time first baseman Daniel Murphy.

After Derek Jeter—newly back from a two-game absence with the flu—doubled to lead off the game, Murphy tried to get Jeter at third base on an infield dribbler by the next hitter, Nick Swisher.

Murphy's throw was ill-advised and very late, and Hernandez appeared rattled by the mistake. He proceeded to give up a two-run double to the ensuing batter, Mark Teixeira, before Jorge Posada's sacrifice fly put the Mets in a 3–0 hole.

Hernandez (5–3) recovered to pitch seven strong innings, not allowing a hit over his final six frames despite walking five overall. But considering the Mets had scored one run in their previous 22 innings since Thursday and were missing Ryan Church due to the flu, that three-run deficit looked insurmountable.

"We have to find some offense somewhere," Manuel said. "There's a lot of things going wrong right now that we've got to get squared away." ∎

The finale of the second Subway Series of the year was a memorable one for Mariano Rivera: not only did he become just the second pitcher in history to record 500 saves, he also batted in his first run on a bases-loaded walk.

Mariano gets 500ᵗʰ save to cap Subway sweep

June 28, 2009 • By Joel Sherman

A crisis had arisen. Tying run on base. Winning run, too. Two out. Eighth inning. Visiting ballpark. It is a trepidatious moment in baseball. But not for the Yankees. Not for a long time. Not with Mariano Rivera around. With the Yankees, this has actually become a moment of serenity.

"You know you are going to get the right guy," Joe Girardi said in describing the peacefulness he experiences calling for Rivera.

Girardi was the catcher on May 17, 1996, when Rivera, filling in for the injured John Wetteland, induced a double-play grounder from Garret Anderson. That finished a Yankees win that gave Rivera save No. 1 in his career.

And Girardi, now the Yankees manager, summoned him into this crisis at Citi Field. Rivera now had 499 saves. He also had David Wright and Fernando Tatis on base, walked there by Brian Bruney. The Yankees led just 3–2. For the Yankees to win and complete this Subway Series sweep, Rivera would have to produce the 110ᵗʰ save of his career of more than three outs.

"You know what I was thinking," Alex Rodriguez said of watching Rivera move toward the mound, "I was thinking what an honor and privilege it was to be on the field right then."

When Rivera registered that first save 13 years ago, he had more hair but did not yet possess his signature cutter. Instead, in 1996, he relied almost exclusively on a placid delivery that lulled hitters before—boom—menacing four-seam fastballs whooshed by at the top of the zone. It was when he became a full-time closer that he developed the cutter.

And here he was at the brink of history, full count on Omir Santos, and he throws what Andy Pettitte called Rivera's "best cutter of the season." It was a 92 mph dart that started about a half foot off the plate inside before taking a late veer over the corner. Santos was frozen. Strike 3.

Brilliant precision. Crisis averted. Again.

"He's amazing," Pettitte said.

That feeling only grew in the top of the ninth. Francisco Rodriguez was ordered to intentionally walk Derek Jeter to load the bases with two outs. That is because Rivera was on deck. Rivera has only two at-bats in his career. But he worked the count full. And unlike Rivera in the bottom of the previous inning, K-Rod could not execute. Rodriguez fired a fastball up and in for ball four. Rivera had the first RBI of his Career; he had delivered an insurance run to himself for the first time.

He smiled. And then he went back to his real job. Daniel Murphy singled with two outs in the ninth. Alex Cora was the tying run. But Rivera needed just one more pitch, a cutter of course, to get Cora to ground meekly to second. The Yankees had a 4–2 victory and their sweep at Citi Field. Rivera had his 500ᵗʰ save, joining Trevor Hoffman as the only relievers in history to reach the milestone.

"I didn't expect any of this," Rivera said afterward. How could anyone expect it? He barely made the team in 1996. But slowly—with one success after another—he gained then-manager Joe Torre's trust and moved from mop-up to long man to main set-up guy to Wetteland's fill-in on that May night.

It would be the first of his 230 saves at the old Stadium, and last night would be his first at Citi Field, his 27ᵗʰ different stadium with a save. Last night was memorable, first RBI and 500th save, but Rivera hardly seems done, at least when it comes to saves.

He has 18 on the season (in 19 tries). In his last four games, he has four saves, four innings, one hit, no walks, seven strikeouts. He was brilliant on May 17, 1996. He still is. He is not stopping at 500. There are more crises ahead. More serenity for Rivera to deliver. ∎

Since taking over for John Wetteland in 1996, there's been no more dominant closer than Mariano Rivera. From his dominating cutter to unequaled playoff success, there may have been none better in the history of the game. The best part is that he's still going strong.

Rivera has played for one team in his career, and sees his career ending in pinstripes.

Q&A

Mariano Rivera

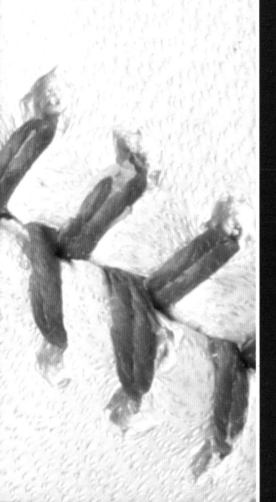

The Post's Steve Serby chatted with the great Yankees closer about his winning legacy, his plans for the rest of his career, his family, and more.

Q: How much longer do you want to play?

A: I have a contract for next year, and after that I don't know what's gonna happen.

Q: You'll still want to play?

A: I want to be successful, so I don't know what's gonna happen. I only can tell you what I know now. I know now I have a contract for next year.

Q: Do you want to retire a Yankee?

A: Definitely.

Q: You want to be one of those players who played for one team his entire career.

A: You got it right.

Q: What's so great about being a New York Yankee?

A: You're playing for the best team in history, period.

Q: One more Yankee contract?

A: I don't say that....I can't tell you that. I have a contract for one more year and after that, I don't know what's gonna happen....I don't know if they want me after that.

Q: During your last contract negotiations, were you close to leaving the Yankees to play for Joe Torre's Dodgers?

A: No.

Q: You were confident you and the Yankees would agree on a (three-year, $45 million) contract?

A: Yes.

Q: What would you say to Yankees fans who are dreading the day when the ninth inning belongs to someone else?

A: I know for sure I'm not gonna do that job forever. I know they know....I don't even have to worry about that. Players come and go.

Q: What would you want written on your (Monument Park) plaque?

A: I want the legacy I left to impact the new guys. I tried to do my best.

Q: One reason, other than your faith in God, why you have been so successful.

A: First of all, support from my family—from my wife (Ciara), my kids (sons Mariano Jr., Jafet and Jaziel)—they've been there for me, and then you have to work hard and take care of yourself.

Q: Do you fear turning 40 in three months?

A: I don't fear it at all—why should I fear turning 40?

Q: As you've gotten older, have you changed your training?

A: Definitely. You get a little older, you train differently. Everything you do, you do more than you did 15 years ago.

Q: The last time you were nervous on the mound?

Melky takes Yanks for a ride on his "cycle"

August 2, 2009 • By George A. King III

They begged CC Sabathia to stop the river of blood racing through the Yankees' universe that threatened to flush them out of the AL East lead. Instead it was Melky Cabrera who applied the tourniquet by hitting for the cycle.

Sabathia pitched well in the clutch yesterday, but without the switch-hitting Cabrera's wood the Yankees don't walk out of U.S. Cellular Field with a colossal 8–5 victory over the White Sox that avoided a four-game sweep.

Pressed into everyday work in center field when Brett Gardner went down July 25, Cabrera (4-for-5, four RBIs) has responded well and raised his average to .292.

"It doesn't matter where I Play; I play hard," said Cabrera, who hit a three-run homer in the second inning off Mark Buehrle (11–5), doubled and scored in the fourth, singled in a run in the fifth and tripled and scored in the ninth.

Cabrera's cycle was the 15th in Yankee history and the first since Tony Fernandez's in 1995.

"When I saw the ball go over (right fielder) Jermaine Dye's head, I knew I had a chance," Cabrera said of the triple that was finished by a slide that just beat the relay throw and resulted in his teammates applauding from the top step of the dugout.

The victory sent the Yankees to Toronto one-half game ahead of the second-place Red Sox in the AL East.

After games with the Blue Jays tomorrow, when Roy Halladay hurls for the hosts, and Wednesday night, when the Yankees have no option but to start the struggling Sergio Mitre, the Yanks open a crucial four-game series against the Red Sox at Yankee Stadium on Thursday evening.

Mariano Rivera posted his 30th save by recording the final four outs. He is tied for the AL save lead.

Cabrera's performance at the plate overshadowed Sabathia's efforts in the clutch. Even though he flushed the 3–0 lead Cabrera gave him in the third by giving up four in the home half, Sabathia held the White Sox to one hit in nine at-bats with runners in scoring position.

"You want to be the guy who the guys think gives you a chance to win," said Sabathia, who improved to 11–7. In seven-plus innings, Sabathia gave up five runs and 10 hits.

The four-run inning that featured back-to-back homers by Dye and Jim Thome was the beginning of the end for the White Sox's success against the big lefty.

He retired eight of the next nine, and in the seventh, with the Yankees leading 7–4, Sabathia didn't let Chris Getz' leadoff triple turn into a run.

"I felt better than I had in the last couple of games," said Sabathia, who fanned Jayson Nix, induced Ramon Castro to ground out and caught Scott Podsednik's infield pop to strand Getz and give the Yankees a big boost.

Phil Hughes picked up Sabathia in the eighth after Gordon Beckham opened with a double. Hughes surfaced to fan Dye, walk Thome and catch Paul Konerko looking. Rivera came in and gave up an RBI single to Carlos Quentin and fanned Getz looking.

"You never want to get swept," Sabathia said. "We still have the lead (over the Red Sox), and we want to keep it." Thanks to Cabrera, they did. ∎

One hallmark of a great team is different players stepping up at different times. On this day in Chicago, it was Melky Cabrera who threw the Yankees on his back.

"The Yankee," now & forever

September 11, 2009 • By Joel Sherman

Derek Jeter stood at first base and took it all in. The symphony of flashbulbs, the howling love of the fans, a line of congratulatory hugs from teammates. It was 9:23 PM, and Jeter was now clear of Lou Gehrig, alone atop the all-time Yankees hit list. A penthouse for one.

This was one of those milestone moments that motivates reflection. It makes you look back to again honor Gehrig. But mainly to remember all of those Jeter hits—that relentless storm of hits.

However, this also was just as much about the future, about a continuing march. Toward 3,000 hits and maybe 4,000. Toward Cooperstown and Monument Park. And toward Jeter becoming "The Yankee" for the rest of his life, the guy who when retirement finally does come, represents an entire era. The guy who on Old-Timers' Day is called last, a designation of affection and respect. Think Joe DiMaggio and Mickey Mantle and...Jeter. It is a strange space that Jeter now occupies, living legend, yet still-thriving star. This is not Mantle circa 1967, when the applause was for a career well done. This is not emeritus love. Jeter is probably going to finish in the top five in the AL MVP voting in 2009.

"I don't think Derek has ever played better than right now," Alex Rodriguez said.

As if to emphasize that point, Jeter followed his historic hit with yet another hard single to right in his next at-bat, hit No. 2,723. So he already is pulling away from Gehrig, one behind Roberto Alomar for 52nd all-time. Somewhere up in the distance are Ty Cobb and Pete Rose. Somewhere up in the distance is a rest of a life as "The Yankee."

For now though, he is No. 1 on the team's all-time hit list. No. 1 with a bullet. Because he is going to be holding the top spot for quite a while. For Jeter is hitting .330. Rodriguez says it feels like the Yankee shortstop gets three hits every day. A-Rod called him "a robot."

This was a pause for celebration and honor. But Jeter is continuing. He is going to make the mountain higher for some next great Yankee to reach, higher than the Gehrig peak. Somebody not yet born may have to accumulate 3,500 or more hits to get into the Yankees conversation with Jeter. What made his moment particularly riveting was that it was not charity. This was not Denny McLain serving up a meatball so Mantle could pass Jimmie Foxx in the twilight. Jeter did not do this limping, broken, faltering.

Leading off the third inning, Jeter lashed a 90-plus-mph Chris Tillman fastball on one screaming hop between Luke Scott and the first-base bag. Jeter was surprised how many fans stuck around through an 87-minute rain delay and a constant downpour during the action. But there they were. The already-standing crowd of 46,771 intensified both the noise and adoration. One of the two key magic numbers in this overwhelming Yankees season was now reached, and that magic number was 2,722.

Jeter acknowledged the crowd, his teammates, his parents. For the second time in three days, Jeter was told in the loudest, clearest way possible where he stands. And not just in the moment. Of course, he wants more championships to go along with the boatload of hits still ahead of him. But with or without those rings, Jeter's pinstripe status is understood. He came along, and the Canyon of Heroes opened up to the Yankees again. He served with Mariano Rivera as the cornerstone to a dynasty and did it with dignity and capability. He represents what Yankees fans want to idealize about their team, not only extreme effectiveness, but the ability to rise with huge moments and to do it all with a streak of humility.

For that, he soaked in the love on a rainy night. He heard what the crowd thinks of him again. He reached a milestone. But there were no stop signs. It is 2,723—and counting. ∎

He's not a hobbled, graying former star holding on for just a few more hits. Derek Jeter may be plowing through Yankee records, but he's still at the top of his game—a long way away from saying good-bye.

Just like Jeter

September 11, 2009 • By Larry Brooks

No single player is bigger than the game, but last night's Yankees-Orioles game in The Bronx was about one player. Last night's game was about Derek Jeter. Check that. No it wasn't. Last night's game was about two players. It was about Jeter and Lou Gehrig. But it was more than that, too. Last night's game was about history. It was about an appointment to history. And it was accepted by the Yankees captain, who not only could have played for any team (well, post-1947) in franchise history, but is the perfect linear descendent to Gehrig, the first Yankees captain.

History and an immediately updated Yankeeography will record that career hit number 2,722—one more than Gehrig amassed, a couple of hundred more than Babe Ruth recorded, and considerably more than any other player to wear the interlocking NY—came at 9:23 PM on a third-inning leadoff single inside the first-base bag.

The 2–0 opposite-field smash off Baltimore rookie right-hander Chris Tillman, which eluded Luke Scott's dive, was nearly a carbon copy of the hit that tied the Iron Horse's mark on Wednesday against the Rays. It was signature Jeter, head down, inside-out swing, eye on the ball, eyes on the prize.

The ovation swelled from the crowd of 46,771 strong that chanted "Der-ek Jet-er" in roll-call style before the game, again during his first-inning strikeout and then as he both stepped to the plate for his historic at-bat and soon after as he stood at first, alone on the mountaintop.

The Yankees left the dugout en masse to congratulate Jeter. Teammates embraced the captain. Jeter doffed his helmet to the crowd. He pointed to the suite where his parents, Charles and Dorothy Jeter, and his family and friends were witness to the occasion. The roars grew louder.

"When my teammates came out, that surprised me. It caught me off guard, and I didn't know what to do," Jeter said close to 1 a.m., nearly three-and-a-half hours after a 67-minute rain delay, which followed an 87-minute pregame delay. "It was a special moment for me and for the organization.

"What I'll remember first and foremost was the fans. I didn't know how many would be here after the (first) delay. For the fans to stick around means a lot. The whole experience has been overwhelming. It's still hard for me to believe."

His next at-bat, he drove another single to right, knocking in his team's final run of the night in the 10–4 defeat.

"Fifty years from now people will look at the back of his baseball card and see a crazy number of hits, but that won't even capture 50 percent of it," Alex Rodriguez said in the wee hours as he, Jorge Posada and Andy Pettitte delivered remarkable testimonials to their teammate that might have come from star-struck fans, such was the verbiage and emotion. "Being able to play next to him and watch him every day is a privilege. He's motivated me and inspired me."

Last night wasn't so much a ballgame as it was appointment baseball. It was an appointment to history that was fulfilled by Jeter this night to remember on which he surpassed an American icon who will never be forgotten. ∎

The hit that pushed Jeter past Gehrig solidified his place in Yankees history—his resume with World Series rings and a track record of leadership and broken records puts him among the best to ever wear the pinstripes.

Jeter is stout and resolute in his response: he has no fear of
Father Time catching up to him. With his track record, he
should have little to fear in the coming seasons.

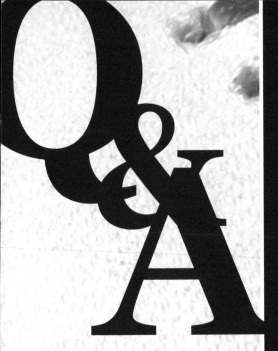

Q&A

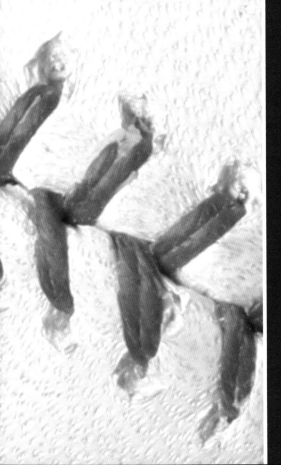

Steve Serby sat down with the Yankees captain for a wide-ranging interview that includes his thoughts on his future with the team, his side interests, the possibility of him ever getting married, and much more.

Derek Jeter

Q: What is so much fun about playing shortstop for the New York Yankees?

A: It's fun because it's been a dream of mine....I just had the opportunity to live out my dream, so that's why it's been so fun for me. This is what I've always wanted to do. I've never wanted to do anything else, therefore it's fun for me, just like I'm sure your dream was to write Serby's Question & Answer on Sunday. Now you're doing it. I'm sure it's fun for you.

Q: From Little League on, that was always my dream.

A: There ya go (laughs).

Q: Can you envision yourself playing another position for the Yankees than shortstop?

A: Can I envision? No.

Q: What if they asked you?

A: You're speaking in hypotheticals.

Q: I know.

A: I can't answer that question.

Q: Anyway, I was listening to the radio, and they were talking about maybe...

A: I don't listen to the radio, so...wherever you're going with that question, I don't even want to hear it.

Q: But your last day as a Yankee, whenever that will be, you want to be at shortstop.

A: You asked me, "Can I envision myself playing another position?" My answer o that question is "No, I can't envision it," so...

Q: You look sleeker.

A: Been the exact same for about the last...eight years.

Q: Have you asked Michael Jordan or anybody about dealing with Father Time?

A: Nope.

Q: You don't fear Father Time?

A: Um, uh, do you?

Q: It's too late for me. Many athletes fear Father Time.

A: No.

Q: It's something you don't even think about?

Unflappable in front of 50,000 fans at Yankee Stadium, Jeter admits to being nervous the first time he talked to George Steinbrenner.

A: How could I help?

Q: You're Derek Jeter.

A: I don't play basketball though.

Q: What advice would you give him?

A: I'd say play where you're happy.

Q: Do you think he'd be happy here?

A: Don't know....I don't know him well enough to answer that.

Q: If he came to New York, would you go the Garden to watch him play?

A: Yeah, I'm sure I would.

Q: Your opinion of (President) Obama so far?

A: I like Obama....I really like the way he carries himself.

Q: What is it about the way he carries himself?

A: He just doesn't seem like he gets flustered too much.

Q: Do you want a large family some day?

A: What's large?

Q: Four.

A: Four kids?

Q: Yeah.

A: Let me work on getting married and having one before I start putting numbers on it.

Q: How close are you?

A: Probably closer than I was the last time I talked to you (chuckles). When was the last time I talked to you?

Q: Last year at this time.

A: You know that's all you're getting from me with that (smiles).

Q: Who do you think the best man will be in your wedding?

A: See I'm not even gonna answer that question, because if I answer that question, then somebody'll take that answer, and they'll say that I'm getting married real soon, and I've announced my best man—trust me, I've seen it happen so...I will not answer that one either.

Q: Have you become more guarded?

A: More? I've always been.

Q: I know you have. But it seems like you've become more.

A: Because now everything's dissected....Everything you say, (they) will take it out of context, they run with it, they make their own stories....I think you should be guarded with what you say.

Q: I will word it in such a way where nobody can confuse the fact that you're not getting married soon. But my other question was could you ever see inviting a Red Sock or a Met to your wedding?

A: Friend of mine, yeah.

Q: Who would you want presenting you at the Hall of Fame?

A: Hall of Fame, man—slow down, buddy. I don't even talk about those kind of things.

Q: Tell me why you miss Bob Sheppard.

A: He was as (much a) part of Yankee Stadium as any player was, I think. He was a part of the whole experience....Coming here as a fan, being here as a player...it just seemed like home when Bob Sheppard's voice was going over the P.A. And that's why to this day when I come up to the plate, it's his voice.

Q: George Steinbrenner (79) had a birthday yesterday. Do you remember the first time you met him, and was it intimidating when you met him?

A: First time I met him I was 18 years old; it was right after I had been drafted....Yeah I was intimidated. You know, he has that presence where he walks in a room, even if you don't know who he is, you know he's somebody....Yeah, I was scared to meet him.

Q: He once said about you, "He's like Jack Armstrong and Frank Merriwell."

A: Anything he says is all right with me (laughs). Can't argue with The Boss, right?

Q: By the way, your fielding percentage this year, you're at a career high.

A: Why would you even say something like that? Now you're trying to jinx me.

Q: Career low then, you're at a career low.

A: (Laughs).

Q: I'm asking you that because I've heard all these things about your range.

A: Once again, I don't pay attention to it.

Q: See, that's the key to New York right there—block everything out.

A: Everyone has an opinion.

Q: You've worked on your lateral movement a lot?

A: I feel good, feel good this year.

Q: Agility-wise?

A: Yeah.

Q: Better than last year?

A: Feel good.

Q: What do you listen to on your way to the stadium?

A: Hip hop, R&B.

Q: Dancing With the Stars?

A: Never. I wouldn't embarrass myself like that....I've embarrassed myself before, but I wouldn't embarrass myself dancing like that.

Q: You hosted Saturday Night Live...

A: I wasn't dancin' though.

Q: The Delta Batting Challenge?

A: It's a little competition we got, for my Foundation and David Wright's Foundation.

Q: 100G for higher batting average, 50G for runner-up. So he's in the lead.

A: It's a long season.

Q: Do you think he is—or will be—a good leader?

A: I think he is. I had the opportunity to get to know him a little bit during the WBC....I think he's doing a great job over there...and one thing you gotta learn is people are always gonna say this or say that. I think he needs to continue doing what he's doing. I think he's doing a great job.

Q: You're not far behind Rickey Henderson on the all-time Yankee-stolen-base list.

A: Is that right? Did not know that.

Q: You may end up with a career high in stolen bases this year, too.

A: You're really trying to jinx everything that's going on.

Q: Do you keep a book on pitchers?

A: Nope, not at all.

Q: What's your key to stealing bases?

A: If you think you can make it, run. If you don't, stay.

Q: What are the odds you will retire as a Yankee?

A: I would like to.

Q: Do you expect to?

A: I would like to. You learn not to expect too many things. I'd like to, but the decision's not entirely up to me, I don't think (chuckles). ∎

Bombers follow A-Rod's lead

September 27, 2009 • By Joel Sherman

Alex Rodriguez is the Yankees, and the Yankees are Alex Rodriguez. Rodriguez has never symbolized the team more than now. He is the richest player on the richest team. He is most talented and most despised, just like the Yankees. Like so many teammates, Rodriguez is thirtysomething and battling back from physical maladies.

And after so many empty Octobers, both Rodriguez and the Yankees again will try to enhance their postseason reputations.

But if you want to believe that the playoffs will be different this time for the largest personality and biggest team, then focus on how the hugest collection of stars became a cohesive galaxy.

Off-season acquisitions Mark Teixeira, CC Sabathia, A.J. Burnett and Nick Swisher brought not only substantial talent, but also personalities that enhanced the bonhomie of the group. Manager Joe Girardi preached unity over individualism, and the roster pretty much bought into a positivism that helped buoy spirits even when the Red Sox opened 8–0 against the Yankees.

No player needed to be blanketed in such an atmosphere more than Rodriguez. And no one needed to buy into the concept more than a player both humiliated and debilitated before ever taking a meaningful swing in 2009. To his credit, Rodriguez stopped making it about him and melded more into the group.

That is why he was soaked and squinting through the sting of champagne late yesterday afternoon as he said, "It has been a special year." That's true for both Rodriguez and the team he so epitomizes.   The Yankees did not wilt at 0–8 against the Red Sox. These Yankees stayed upbeat, honored their talent, and became a regular-season wrecking ball destroying all in their path. On this final weekend of September, it was again the Red Sox who were flattened. The Yankees completed a three-game sweep with a 4–2 victory that incredibly evened the season series at 9–9 while clinching both the AL East and the majors' best record.

Andy Pettitte pitched six strong innings for his 14th win, and Hideki Matsui reached 90 RBIs by delivering a two-out, two-run single in the sixth to put the Yanks ahead. They were two of the thirtysomethings returning from injury. Teixeira homered for insurance in the eighth inning. That gave the most expensive position player signed in the offseason 120 RBIs, a day after the most expensive pitcher signed in the offseason, Sabathia, won his 19th game.

But the key at-bat belonged to A-Rod. Behind Paul Byrd 0–2 with two out and one on in the sixth, Rodriguez battled and battled—kind of like he did to simply get back on the field this year—and on the 10th pitch lashed a single to center to knock out Byrd. Matsui followed with his decisive single off Takashi Saito. "When Alex came back to our lineup, our lineup started rolling," Pettitte said.

The Yankees were 13–15 when Rodriguez was disabled and are 87–41 since. It is no accident. "It is tough to do what they have done, especially since Alex came back," Boston manager Terry Francona said.

Rodriguez has been a difference-making force batting cleanup—amazing because he had a nightmare while recovering from hip surgery in Colorado that he would never play at all this year.

At that moment, he had the tabloid disgrace that was his 2008 season, a steroid revelation that soiled his legacy and hip surgery that threatened his career. So Rodriguez decided to embrace the group, to play for joy. That helped displace the tension, and a symbiotic relationship was formed in which the team defused pressure on Rodriguez, and A-Rod's elite skill made it easier for everyone around him to thrive.

That mutual cooperation led to a celebration that washed across the clubhouse yesterday. Maybe that will all dissolve into familiar recriminations with a Rodriguez 0-for-4 in AL Division Series Game 1, coupled with a Yankees loss. Or maybe this finally will be the year that both star and star-infused team can relax and thrive in October.

"I have been through hell and back," Rodriguez said.

Can you get to the Canyon of Heroes from hell? ■

It's no secret that adding a three-time MVP to the cleanup spot in the order will change a team's complexion. Still, the Yankees had no idea that their improvement once Alex Rodriguez returned was going to be quite so drastic.

Mark Teixiera had one thing in mind
once he finally donned the pinstripes:
winning a World Series.

Q&A

The Post's Steve Serby chatted with the Yankees' new $180-million first baseman about having been teammates with both A-Rod and K-Rod, his idolization of Don Mattingly, his family life, and much more.

Mark Teixeira

Q: Since you spurned the Red Sox, what do you expect the Fenway reaction to you will be?

A: I would expect they would boo me. I wouldn't expect anything less. I'd be disappointed if I didn't get booed.

Q: What would your message to Yankee fans be about Mark Teixeira and winning a World Series?

A: I'm not gonna be satisfied until we bring home a championship to the new Yankee Stadium.

Q: Do you burn to win a World Series?

A: That's the only goal in my career right now.

Q: What do you expect from yourself?

A: I don't settle for "just good enough."

Q: Playing in New York?

A: I think you just need to be comfortable with yourself, comfortable talking with the media and talking with the fans. I love big crowds. I love playing in front of 50,000 screaming fans.

Q: Becoming a Gold Glove first baseman?

A: It came very naturally to me. I wasn't a very good third baseman. My rookie year I got switched over to first. I was meant to play first all along.

Q: What drives you?

A: Fear of failure. Every competitor wants to succeed....You can never be good enough in baseball.

Q: What makes CC Sabathia so tough?

A: He's got great stuff, and he's huge. He hides the ball real well because of his size.

Q: A.J. Burnett?

A: His fastball has another level to it. It comes out of his hand, by the time you swing it's already by you.

Q: You played with Francisco Rodriguez in Anaheim. What will he mean to the Mets?

From a young age, Teixiera had an appreciation for the Yankees, especially the Stadium and Don Mattingly.

A: I think he's gonna be huge. He's closed so many big games. He wants the ball in that ninth inning. I think the Mets are gonna win a lot more—the ninth inning is gonna be shut down.

Q: Mariano Rivera, with that cutter, was the last pitcher you wanted to face?

A: Even though you know it's coming, it's so hard to hit.

Q: Alex Rodriguez in Texas?

A: He was great for me to see as a rookie. I got a chance to see the best player in baseball.

Q: Derek Jeter?

A: Just the consummate professional. He's friendly with all his teammates. He's great with the media, great with the fans...he's The Captain.

Q: Compare Joe Girardi and (Angels manager) Mike Scioscia.

A: Obviously, being catchers, they're captain of the team behind the plate. That's kind of the way they manage their ballclubs. They're very prepared. They're very keen on the small things in baseball that win games.

Q: Why was Don Mattingly your idol?

A: I can't put my finger on one thing...his sweet swing...the way he played defense...the pinstripes...I just think he had it all.

Q: You wear No. 25. Do you miss the No. 23 you wore at Georgia Tech and Texas?

A: I do. I also recognize there's a special No. 23 in Yankee history. Even if it wasn't retired, I wouldn't wear it.

Q: The first time you met Mattingly?

A: Legends Field in Tampa at spring training (2002). We (Rangers) just played the Yankees. I went up to him and introduced myself. I told him I was a huge fan. We had a three, four minute conversation. It was great.

Q: Home Run Derby as a kid?

A: It was Wiffle ball. We had a blast. That's how I started switch-hitting.

Q: Did you pretend you were Mattingly?

A: Whenever I was left-handed I was Mattingly. Cal Ripken was No. 1 on my list when I hit right-handed.

Q: Your son Jack is 3.

A: He's not gonna be able to recite the entire Yankee lineup yet. He definitely knows I play baseball.

Q: Describe him.

A: High energy. He's just like his dad, the same way I was when I was a kid. He loves to jump off couches, loves to wrestle. He does it all.

Q: Your daughter Addison is 16 months old.

A: She's a lot more calm. She's learned to fight back—Jack's always wrestling with her.

Q: Do you change diapers?

A: Not often. But in the off-season, when my wife needs me to, I'm definitely there.

Q: Are you any good?

A: Oh yeah. I've changed enough. I know exactly what I'm doing.

Q: Favorite childhood memory?

A: I was in fifth grade; I got my dog for Christmas.

Q: What kind of dog?

A: A West Highland white terrier.

Q: What did you name it?

A: McKenzie.

Q: Why not Mattingly?

A: That's a little too predictable.

Q: Your father was a navy pilot.

A: He was very strict on me growing up. I knew right and wrong from a very young age. He was my Little League coach—he taught me how to play ball in the backyard. He taught me how to switch-hit.

Q: Best piece of advice he gave you?

A: He told me I was given a gift. I should work as hard as I can to get the most out of it.

Q: The first time you saw Yankee Stadium?

A: I was 9 or 10 years old. My dad took me to a game to watch Mattingly play. It was larger than life. Even at a young age, I appreciated the history of it.

Q: Favorite golf course?

A: Augusta National. I've had a chance to play it a few times. It definitely takes the cake.

Q: What did you shoot?

A: 88, 92, 87.

Q: Favorite New York City things?

A: Restaurants—Uncle Jack's Steakhouse, Tanzen.

Q: Three dinner guests?

A: Jesus Christ, George Washington, Will Ferrell.

Q: Favorite movie?

A: *The Godfather.*

Q: Favorite actor?

A: Pacino.

Q: Favorite actress?

A: Reese Witherspoon.

Q: Favorite entertainer?

A: George Strait.

Q: Favorite meal?

A: Surf and turf.

Bombers rally to win Game 1

October 7, 2009 • By George A. King III

Ron Gardenhire manages Joe Mauer, so he recognizes studs when he sees them. Last night in Game 1 of the ALDS at Yankee Stadium the Twins' manager saw them almost everywhere he looked in the Yankees' lineup.

"Everyone is a stinking All-Star," the Twins' manager said of the Yankees hitters.

The Steinbrenner Family All-Stars were no match for the physically shot and emotionally spent Twins, who lost the opener of the best-of-five series, 7–2, in front of a sold-out gathering of 49,464 in the first playoff opener at the new Stadium.

Asked if his AL Central champs, who needed 12 innings Tuesday to beat the Tigers 6–5 in a tiebreaker game at home, were fatigued, Gardenhire said there were other forces working against the Twins.

"I kind of think it was CC Sabathia stress," Gardenhire said of the Yankees' ace, who gave up two runs (one earned) in the third and nothing else in 6 ⅔ innings.

Sabathia's first taste of the postseason in a Yankees uniform was supported by a lineup that produced five two-out RBIs and was kick started by Derek Jeter's two-out, two-run homer off Brian Duensing in the third that tied the score, 2–2.

"Once the lights hit the postseason, it's Jeter time," said Nick Swisher, whose two-out double scored Robinson Cano from first in the fourth to put the Yankees ahead, 3–2.

Adding to the festive atmosphere was Alex Rodriguez breaking out of a postseason slump with runners in scoring position and Hideki Matsui's two-run, two-out homer in the three-run fifth.

Rodriguez, who started the game hitless in the last 18 at-bats with runners in scoring position, drove in runs with singles in the fifth and seventh with runners in scoring position.

With Rodriguez breaking out and Sabathia evening his postseason record at 3–3, the talk of them not being able to deliver in the second season dissipated.

"We don't listen to it, so if somebody said that I don't think too many people were talking about it in the clubhouse," said Jeter, who went 2-for-2, scored three runs, drove in two and walked twice. "We wanted to play well as a group. We did a lot of good things today."

The Yankees' eighth straight win over the Twins this year gives them an early advantage in the best-of-five series that continues tomorrow night at the Stadium, where A.J. Burnett faces Nate Blackburn in Game 2.

Leading, 3–2, the Yankees scored three in the fifth to take command of the game. Rodriguez's RBI single was followed by Matsui's homer to center field. It was Matsui's 11th homer this year in games Sabathia starts.

After Sabathia exited to a standing ovation that he responded to by tipping his cap, Phil Hughes, Phil Coke, Joba Chamberlain and Mariano Rivera provided 2 ⅓ innings of scoreless relief. None of the four runners inherited by the bullpen scored.

With a 1–0 lead, the Yankees don't have to stew over being in an early hole, and they have Jeter to thank for that.

"It's pretty fitting what he did tonight," manager Joe Girardi said of Jeter, who led off the first inning with a single and homered two innings later. "That's Derek Jeter this time of the year." ■

CC Sabathia was able to tip his hat to the crowd at Yankee Stadium after an impressive performance against the clearly overmatched and exhausted Minnesota Twins. He scattered eight hits and just one of Minnesota's runs was earned.

Tex, A-Rod have blasts in wild ALDS win

October 9, 2009 • By George A. King III

Mystique, aura and the ghosts have taken up residence in the latest Yankee Stadium. How else can you explain last night's 4–3, 11-inning victory over the Twins in Game 2 of the ALDS?

First, Alex Rodriguez tied the score, 3–3, with a two-run homer in the ninth off closer Joe Nathan; then, Mark Teixeira won it by tucking a searing line drive inside the left-field foul pole leading off the 11th.

And those two events were mainstream compared with David Robertson escaping a bases-loaded, no-out jam in the 11th and left-field umpire Phil Cuzzi incorrectly calling Joe Mauer's leadoff fly ball to left in the inning foul.

"That was crazy. Are you kidding me?" CC Sabathia said after the Yankees grabbed a 2–0 lead in the best-of-five series and headed for Minneapolis, where Game 3 will be played tomorrow night.

Informed that those types of wins used to happen often across the street, Sabathia said, "That's what (Andy) Pettitte told me."

Derek Jeter, who scored the Yankees' first run in the sixth, has spoken often about bringing the ghosts across 161st Street.

"(The ghosts) have been showing up all year," Jeter said, referring to the 15 walk-off victories in the regular season.

Trailing, 3–1, going to the ninth, Teixeira opened with a single before Rodriguez crushed a 3–1 middle-of-the-plate fastball into the Yankees' bullpen to tie the score.

"It just felt really good; obviously we needed it," said Rodriguez, who also drove in Jeter with a two-out single in the sixth. "There has been a lot of magic, and everybody has contributed. For me personally, that was obviously a lot of fun, and I enjoyed it."

In the top of the 11th, Damaso Marte almost threw an ocean of cold water on the pebbled skin of the 50,006 in the crowd. After Cuzzi botched the call on what would have been a ground-rule double by Mauer, the AL batting champion singled to center. Jason Kubel, 0-for-5 with three strikeouts to that point, followed with a single.

That was enough for manager Joe Girardi. He called for Robertson, who surrendered a single to Michael Cuddyer that loaded the bases.

Robertson rebounded by getting Delmon Young on a liner to Teixeira, inducing Carlos Gomez to force Mauer at the plate with a grounder to Teixeira and watching Brendan Harris lift a harmless fly to center field.

"We called it the Houdini act," Jeter said of Robertson's escape.

As for the blown call, crew chief Tim Tschida admitted Cuzzi blew it.

"We went in and looked at It, and it's a clear indication that an incorrect decision was rendered," Tschida said.

Though the call was wrong, the Twins had the bases juiced and didn't score.

Everybody wants to get out of that situation. I was just glad to get out of it," said Robertson, whose first taste of the postseason will be hard to forget.

The Yankees missed a chance to win the game in the 10th when Jorge Posada singled with one out and pinch runner Brett Gardner—who stole second and went to third on a bad throw by Twins closer Joe Nathan—broke from third on Johnny Damon's one-out liner to short and was doubled off for the final out.

An inning later, Teixeira ushered in more ghosts.

"I really thought it was going to be a double because I hit it with so much top-spin," said Teixeira, whose ninth-inning single stopped an 0-for-7 slide. "I thought there was no chance it was going to get out." ∎

The Yankees' big guns proved their mettle during the tense moments of Game 2. There are few relievers tougher than Minnesota's Joe Nathan, but Alex Rodriguez was able to school the Twins hurler with his ninth-inning homer.

Past echoes mix with new cheers

October 9, 2009 • By Mike Vaccaro

As it turns out, Sinatra sounds just as sweet in the new place. The walls rattle and shake with the same fevered fervor, and the new foundation can be battered to its core, and the air can be filled with grandiose glee that thunders down all the way from the upper deck. And even the old ghosts are welcome, billed as very special guest stars.

"As much as you think you know what it's like here," a kid pitcher named David Robertson said, wide-eyed and wonder-filled, "you don't know until you see it. And then it's so much better than you could ever have imagined."

Last night was for the newbies, and it was for the old-timers who had wondered all year if any of the old magic had been shoved across 161st Street. It was for an old superstar named Alex Rodriguez, suddenly liberated from his past, the shackles officially loosened from his bat, and for a new ascendant star, Mark Teixeira, who put a ball in the seats and got a pie in the face for his troubles.

It was for all of them, this sparkling, 4–3, 11-inning victory that vaults them halfway across the country up two games to none in this best-of-five ALDS. It was for the 50,006 people crammed into the stands, an old-school October crowd that crackled with life all across the night.

"It was a great, great game to be a part of," said Jose Molina, although on the other end of the corridor, a crushed band of Minnesota Twins begged to differ.

"It's disappointing," Twins manager Ron Gardenhire said. "I've been walked-off enough times here."

It happened to him three times in an early season series back in May. And it happened again last night, his team stepping on one too many banana peels, allowing the Yankees one extra breath too many. Carlos Gomez cost them a run when he overran second base in the fourth inning. Joe Nathan, an All-Star closer, couldn't hold a two-run lead in the ninth and served up a fat fastball that Rodriguez blasted toward the ionosphere.

Later, there would be an atrocious umpire's call, but one the Twins seemed a bit too eager to seize given that they still had bases-loaded, none out a few moments later and couldn't get even one run across...and given that they landed in the playoffs in the first place as the beneficiary of a blown call four days ago.

Then, at last, at the end, there was one last swing, Teixeira getting his first good look at Jose Mijaris and bludgeoning a baseball just over the left-field fence.

"I was running hard, making sure I got (a double)," Teixeira said later, after he had toweled off the remnants of A.J. Burnett's postgame cream-pie greeting. "And then, when the crowd started to go nuts, I figured it was a home run."

He figured right, then he pierced the night with his right fist, and he took himself on one of the grandest tours in sports, the one that takes you around a basepath in The Bronx. It isn't the one that all the ghosts and all the goblins used for all those years, but that hardly matters any longer. This place will do. This place works.

This place is home.

Sinatra was back, his vagabond shoes still longing to stray. The folks in the stands? There may be 6,000 or so fewer than there used to be, but they're all the way back, too, filling every seat again, engaged in every moment, pleading with their voices and believing in their guts.

Now it is all about the baseball team, which spent six months tormenting all comers at home, ripping their way through opposing closers, stealing games in the ninth inning all across the summer. There was a time when there was no harder chore in sports than getting 27 October outs against the Yankees, when they would chase you to the very last strike and beyond.

"You don't always have to score early," Teixeira said, "you just have to score enough."

Words to live by in the Yankees' new house, one that feels just as comfortable and cozy as the old one all of a sudden. ∎

After a summer of stealing games in the final moments, it was only appropriate that the Yankees kept eking out dramatic wins in the fall. Mark Teixeira had been slumping until a ninth-inning single—his walk-off homer in the 11th proved that he was right at home in the postseason.

A-Rod, Andy end Bombers' ALCS drought

October 11, 2009 • By George A. King III

Alex Rodriguez wrapped his dock rope of a left arm around Derek Jeter's neck and let out a howl right before the best player in pinstripes showered the smartest in champagne.

A 4–1 victory over the pesky Twins in Game 3 of the ALDS had propelled the Yankees into the ALCS that starts Friday night in The Bronx against the Angels.

Shortly after the sweep, bedlam broke out in the clubhouse, which is barely bigger than a suburban two-car garage. Though some Yankees fans believe it's their birth right to win the World Series every year, the players understand the difficulty of winning and advancing.

And a big reason was Rodriguez, who supported a pitching gem by Andy Pettitte with an opposite-field homer to right-center in the seventh off Carl "American Idle" Pavano that tied the score 1–1. Jorge Posada's opposite-field homer two batters later put the Yankees ahead 2–1.

"We didn't hit except for Alex, collectively," general manager Brian Cashman said of his club that batted .225 for the series and forgot Jeter hitting .400 (4-for-10).

Without Rodriguez, it wouldn't have been that high. He went 5-for-11 (.455) with two homers and six RBIs in three games.

The Yankees are in the ALCS for the first time since 2004, when they won the first three games against the Red Sox and flushed the final four.

Of course, Rodriguez had help. Jeter made an intelligent play in the eighth that cut down Nick Punto rounding third on Denard Span's infield hit behind second. Knowing he didn't have a chance at the fast Span at first, Jeter spotted Punto rounding third and threw to Posada. With Punto on his way back to third, Posada fired a strike and caught Punto by plenty.

Then there was Pettitte, who retired the first dozen Twins before Michael Cuddyer ripped a single to left leading off the fifth. Pettitte gave up a run in the sixth but left two on.

When he fanned Jason Kubel to open the seventh, Joe Girardi replaced Pettitte with Joba Chamberlain. Considering Pettitte had allowed a run, three hits, a walk, fanned seven and threw 81 pitches, it was a bold move.

"Delmon Young had success (9-for-14; .643 coming into the game) against Andy," Girardi said of the move to Chamberlain. "I thought it was time to go to Joba. We liked the matchup. My gut told me to go to Joba."

Chamberlain was greeted by Young's double but retired the next two batters.

Enter Phil Hughes, whose postseason struggles continued when Punto opened the eighth with a double. Hughes was bailed out by Jeter's play behind second. After he retired Orlando Cabrera on a fly to center, Girardi called for Mariano Rivera. He broke Joe Mauer's bat on a ground-out that ended the frame.

When Rivera walked off the mound, the Yankees led 2–1. When he took it for the ninth, the advantage was 4–1 thanks to consecutive bases-loaded singles by Posada and Robinson Cano off Joe Nathan, who inherited a bases-loaded, one-out jam thanks to three walks.

Rivera recorded the final three outs for his MLB-record 35th postseason save.

So now it's the Angels, who eliminated the Yankees in the first round in 2002 and 2005 and whose "Marbles in the Bathtub" style of offense has given the Yankees fits.

"We are good enough to get through this round," Jeter said. "Now it gets more difficult; Anaheim has a great team. This series we couldn't have played better." ■

The Yankees enjoyed some well-deserved smiles on the field and in the clubhouse after finishing a sweep of the tougher-than-they-looked Minnesota Twins. Riding the bats of Jeter and Rodriguez and receiving quality starts from their pitchers, the team was ready to roll into the ALCS.

CC wins battle of aces for 1–0 ALCS lead

October 16, 2009 • By George A. King III

How do you heal baseball frostbite? If you're the Yankees, you apply as many CCs of red-hot pitching as you can.

On a frosty Bronx night that featured a beefy wind dancing in from left field, ace CC Sabathia sizzled, hurling the Yankees to a 4–1 victory over the clumsy Angels in Game 1 of the ALCS that was witnessed by a chilled Yankee Stadium crowd of 49,688.

Game 2 is slated for tonight, weather permitting, when the Yankees can take a commanding lead in the best-of-seven series. A.J. Burnett is scheduled to start for the Yankees and will be opposed by left-hander Joe Saunders.

Sabathia, pitted against John Lackey, proved for the second time this postseason that the Yankees knew what they were doing when they showered the large lefty with $161 million of George Steinbrenner's money last December.

"When he pitches like that, you don't have to score many runs," Mark Teixeira said.

Sabathia, who won Game 1 of the ALDS against the Twins, allowed a run and four hits in eight innings last night. Mariano Rivera recorded the final three outs for his MLB-record 36th postseason save. In two postseason starts for the Yankees, Sabathia is 2–0 and matched his career October victory total from before he donned pinstripes.

"He had it all working tonight," Alex Rodriguez said.

Three Angels errors led to two of the Yankees' four runs being unearned. And a colossal first-inning communication breakdown by third baseman Chone Figgins and shortstop Erick Aybar really cost the Angels.

"We haven't seen our guys crack the door open for a team like we did tonight," Angels manager Mike Scioscia said. "CC pitched a great game, and we cracked the door open."

Hideki Matsui drove in two runs, and Derek Jeter and Rodriguez plated one each.

With the first-pitch temperature at 45 degrees and the wind biting, Robinson Cano, Teixeira, Johnny Damon and Nick Swisher covered their ears with cloth under their hats, but the cold didn't bother Sabathia.

"CC is a bulldog, that's why I tried to recruit him," Angels center fielder Torii Hunter said. "He wasn't cold at all. There is a lot of meat on him. He is a big boy."

Lackey, who worked in short sleeves, was torpedoed by two first-inning miscues. First, left fielder Juan Rivera made a costly throwing error, then Figgins and Aybar watched Matsui's infield pop fall for an RBI single later in the inning.

Lackey hurt himself in the sixth when he walked No. 9 hitter Melky Cabrera with two outs and threw wildly trying to pick him off first. Jeter followed with a single to center that scooted off Hunter's glove, allowing Cabrera to score easily and Jeter to make second.

In 5⅔ innings, Lackey allowed four runs (two earned), nine hits, walked three and fanned three.

The Angels' vaunted marbles-in-the-bathtub attack, which has hurt the Yankees in previous Octobers, was stymied as the Bombers scored twice in the first inning and Figgins, the leadoff hitter, went 0-for-4.

"I was trying to command both sides of the plate and was able to do that early," said Sabathia, who stranded a runner in each of the first two innings. "It opened it up and made the change-up a lot better. So late in the game I went to the change-ups with two strikes. When I needed to get a swing and a miss, the change-up was there for me." ∎

With four hits from the top two batters in the lineup plus a pair of RBIs from Hideki Matsui, CC Sabathia was able to settle into a rhythm and dispatch the Angels on a blustery night at Yankee Stadium.

Cold day in Halo

October 16, 2009 • By Mike Vaccaro

The ball was seemingly a mile high, soaring over the infield, and just for kicks, just for laughs, there had to be a sizable portion of the clientele inside Yankee Stadium and the interested observers at points throughout greater Gotham who instantly heard the same two words careen around their brains: Luis. Castillo.

It was silly, of course. That was early June, and that was the ninth inning and, most relevant, that was the Mets, baseball's endless blooper reel. This was October, the first inning of the American League Championship Series, and these were the Angels, a team we've spent the past five days canonizing as the smartest, savviest kids in class, so sound in fundamentals you can almost see Abner Doubleday and Alexander Cartwright weeping as they watch, saying, "That's how you play our game, lads."

"They are a team that plays the game well and plays the game right, and you don't expect to get any breaks from them," Mark Teixeira said later.

Only, that is precisely what the Yankees were about to get. They already had a run in. They already had a frenzied and frosty crowd percolating behind them. Hideki Matsui lofted the pop-up, and Johnny Damon dutifully sprinted around third and sped toward home, and even if everyone believed this was the most routine kind of play...

Well, they had seen things before, seen things happen at Yankee Stadium before, crazy things, oddball things. And now they saw Chone Figgins, the Angels third baseman, look at Erick Aybar, the shortstop. They saw Aybar look right back at Figgins. They saw the ball twisting in the wind, giving in to gravity.

"It gets awful loud out there," Mike Scioscia, the Angels' manager, explained after the Yankees' 4–1 Game 1 victory, even if he didn't seem terribly convinced by his own rationalization. "And in the weather, the wind can play tricks with the ball..."

It was at this precise moment that Figgins, Aybar, the other 48 players scattered throughout the field, benches and bullpen, and the 49,688 people in the stands, and Scioscia, and manager Joe Girardi, and everyone else started to realize the same thing:

Nobody was going to catch the baseball.

The Yankees were going to take a 2–0 lead.

The Angels had slipped into their Mets uniforms, their Twins uniforms, they had kicked off their spikes and slipped into a pair of banana shoes. The so-called smartest team in baseball suddenly looked dumber than *Brothers*. The so-called savviest team suddenly looked clumsier than Ronan Tynan's sense of humor.

And suddenly, you had to wonder. Maybe it's the Yankees who do all of this, who creep into the Mets' heads in June and the Red Sox's in August and the Twins' in October. Maybe it's Yankee Stadium. Maybe that's the overriding effect of walking into the Stadium and knowing the Yankees aren't ever going to beat themselves, aren't ever going to make it easy for you, and will make you earn every one of the 27 outs you need to collect if you're going to walk off the field happy.

"We cracked the door open for them, and they kept chipping away at it," Scioscia said, before choosing a simpler term to describe what he had just seen: Ugly.

Maybe it was ugly, the same as the Twins series was ugly. Why shouldn't it have been? It was a brutal night, Yankee Stadium playing like Lambeau Field, the wind stealing home runs from both Vladimir Guerrero and Robinson Cano, whipping everyone like Edgar Prado trying to beat it down the backstretch at Belmont.

But the Yankees had CC Sabathia throwing the ball like a hulking poet, and they accepted timely singles and doubles with their home-run strokes grounded, and they watched the Angels turn into a tribute band for Marvelous Marv Throneberry, kicking the ball around and generally looking like Bob Hayes digging his hands in his uniform pants in the Ice Bowl.

"We'll take it," said Damon, who rediscovered his mojo with two hits and two runs.

Sure they will. When someone is offering, as the Angels so generously did last night, as so many spooked teams have all across the summer? You bet they will take it. ∎

In the cold chill of October, a championship team will capitalize on every mistake an opponent makes, turning sure outs into base runners and runs wherever possible. In Game 1, the Yankees did just that, making the most of Angel mistakes—none bigger than the infield's pop-up blunder.

Bombers get 1:00 AM walk-off on Angels' error

October 17, 2009 • By George A. King III

The world's largest walk-in freezer hosted a sizzling baseball game last night. With a biting wind howling from left field making it feel colder than the thermometer read and the much-anticipated piercing rain arriving in the ninth inning, the Yankees and Angels played Game 2 of the ALCS at a frigid Yankee Stadium that was imperfect and riveting. Finally, after five hours, Melky Cabrera's ground ball to second baseman Maicer Izturis was thrown away at second, allowing Jerry Hairston to score from second and lift the Yankees to a pulsating 4–3 victory in front of 49,922 soggy and chilled fans at Yankee Stadium that took 13 innings—and five hours and 10 minutes—to finish.

"As soon as I saw the ball get by the shortstop, I headed for home," said Hairston, who led off the inning with a pinch-hit line single to center and went to second on Brett Gardner's sacrifice bunt.

The win puts the Yankees in a commanding, 2–0 lead in the best-of-seven series that resumes tomorrow at Angel Stadium, where Game 3 will pit Andy Pettitte against Jered Weaver.

Alex Rodriguez's sensational postseason continued when he hit an 0–2 pitch from lefty Brian Fuentes into the right-field seats leading off the 11th to tie the score, 3–3, as the rain intensified.

"At first I thought it was a double or a homer," Rodriguez said of his third postseason homer this year. "I wasn't sure. Once I got the home-run call, I was happy."

The Angels had taken a lead in the top of the 11th off Alfredo Aceves when Gary Matthrews Jr. walked, went to second on Erick Aybar's sacrifice and scored on Chone Figgins' RBI single. It was Figgins' first hit in five postseason games.

After the Yankees jumped to a 2–0 lead on Robinson Cano's RBI triple in the second and Derek Jeter's home run in the third, and the Angels scored twice in the fifth to tie it, the bullpens took over.

Mariano Rivera threw 2⅓ scoreless innings, and Joba Chamberlain left the bases loaded in the seventh. David Robertson worked around a two-out double by Jeff Mathis in the 12th and Robinson Cano's second error on Erick Aybar's lead-off grounder in the 13th.

"We had some relievers with guts," Rodriguez said.

While the game was won in the 13th on an error, it would have ended a lot sooner as a loss if not for Rodriguez's theatrics.

"He's been clutch....He's just doing what he's supposed to do. That doesn't surprise me from him," Rivera said.

"I couldn't believe it, obviously we all know Alex is a great player, but the way he has come up big in the first five games is incredible," Mark Teixeira said.

Starter A.J. Burnett was lifted for lefty Phil Coke after Cano booted Erick Aybar's routine, one-out grounder in the seventh.

Coke came in to face the switch-hitting Figgins, who was 0-for-17 in the postseason. Based on Figgins being a .323 (133-for-412) hitter against righties and .246 (50-for-203) versus lefties in the regular season, the move was the right one for Joe Girardi to make.

However, Coke walked Figgins on a 3–1 pitch. He came back by fanning Abreu, and Girardi immediately called for Chamberlain to face Hunter.

Hunter hit a slow roller to Jeter for an infield single that loaded the bases for Vladimir Guerrero.

When Jose Molina and Chamberlain couldn't agree on an 0–2 pitch, the catcher went to the mound and was joined by Girardi. The decision to use a slider worked, and Guerrero fanned to send Chamberlain into a fist pump and strand three. ■

It's rare that a five-hour game can be so riveting, but the Angels and Yankees played a true classic in Game 2. Alex Rodriguez helped carry the Yankees to extra innings, but in the end it was another miscue from the usually-stout Angel defense that buried the visitors.

Girardi's crew keeps finding ways to win

October 17, 2009 • By Mike Vaccaro

You keep thinking they can't keep this up, that they can't keep filling these playoff nights with this much breathless baseball, that they can't keep pumping out moments and memories like cars on a conveyor belt. You figure one of these nights, manager Joe Girardi will run out of players, the Yankees will run out of outs, and someone will figure out it's not a good idea to throw Alex Rodriguez a strike.

Yet five times now in five games, the Yankees have refused to buckle, refused even to wobble. Five times in five games the Yankees have found a way to do something, to do anything, to make these playoff nights end as perfectly as so many of their summer nights did. They are 5–0 in the playoffs, 2–0 in this American League Championship Series, suddenly only two wins away from the World Series, suddenly just six wins away from reclaiming baseball's snowy summit.

"I had a blast out there tonight," Alex Rodriguez said, after the Yankees' 4–3, 13-inning victory was complete, after he had rescued the Yankees for the second time in a week with an 11th-hour, game-tying homer, after making the game look, again, almost impossibly easy. "That was a great game."

What is becoming clearer and more apparent is that this is a great team and a tough team. It isn't the Orioles the Yankees are doing this to anymore, or the Royals, or the Indians; teams that would walk onto Yankee Stadium's new sod all season long and look outclassed from the first swing of batting practice. This isn't the Twins, who were so happy simply to be a part of the playoffs you half expected them to ask the Yankees for autographs while they were here, to buy souvenirs and take home movies.

No, these are the Angels, the Angels who were supposed to at least be eye-level with the Yankees, who were supposed to be just as smart and just as stamped with winning DNA. The Angels, who took a broom and swept the Red Sox clear out of the division series, who now find themselves heading 3,000 miles home needing to do some serious work to prevent that same ignominy from happening to them.

Last night the Angels, the real ones, reported for work, replacing the imposters who had sleepwalked through Game 1. They pitched well, and they forced the issue and tried to run, and they always seemed one elusive hit away from putting the game away and never got that hit; they were every bit as gritty and every bit as stolid as advertised. And looked every bit the Yankees' equal, even as the night turned frosty, even as the rain started falling in earnest just before midnight struck.

"I wasn't worried about the radar," manager Joe Girardi said with a laugh. "I was worrying about getting three outs at a time." But at the end, in the 310th minute of this epic encounter, in the bottom of the 13th, everything finally caught up to the Angels: the pressure of the ALCS, the hot glare of the remnants of 49,922 fans, and—most tellingly—the weather. Melky Cabrera rolled a slow skidder across the wet grass, and Maicer Izturis misfired on a throw to second, and suddenly Jerry Hairston Jr. was roaring around third.

And even now, the Angels had a chance: Chone Figgins picked the ball up, and it looked like a good throw might get Hairson. But there was no throw: Figgins couldn't grip the ball; it fell and died in the dirt, Hairston stomped on home plate, and all was well again.

"I was running out of bullets," Girardi said, after a night in which he used all but one available reliever (Chad Gaudin) and all but one available position player (Francisco Cervelli) and kept trying to figure out a way to put this one in his briefcase. "I'm sure I'll sleep good on that plane."

They all did, undoubtedly. They have the Angels on the brink, and there is little doubt that the Yankees are enjoying their view a hell of a lot more. ∎

Derek Jeter may have never captained a pluckier team. Just when they looked down and out, the Yanks kept storming back. Whether it was in May or October, the 2009 team had a never-say-die attitude that continually put them in a position to win.

Wacky move to Aceves hands Halos a win

October 19, 2009 • By George A. King III

The Yankees are on the razor's edge of technology when gathering information, but yesterday all those computer printouts buried their chance for a victory over the Angels in Game 3 of the ALCS.

Although reliever David Robertson had registered the first two outs in the 11th inning, manager Joe Girardi traveled the path he had cut into the Angel Stadium field from the dugout to the mound. Girardi already had made the walk four times without a pitching change and on several other occasions to call for a reliever.

Howie Kendrick and Jeff Mathis were the next two hitters in the Angels' order, and according to reports compiled by Yankees scouts, computers, and video, Alfredo Aceves' slider provided a better way to retire them than Robertson's fastball/curveball stuff.

"It's just different kind of stuff against those hitters," Girardi said. "We have all the matchups and all the scouting reports and we felt (Aceves) was a better matchup for us."

Nevertheless, Kendrick smoked a single to center, and Mathis scorched a double to left-center that scored Kendrick from first for a 5–4 win in front of 44,911.

The Yankees still lead the best-of-seven series, 2–1, and will send ace CC Sabathia to the mound on three days' rest tonight for Game 4. He will be opposed by Scott Kazmir.

Was Robertson surprised to get the hook?

"A little bit," he said. "But (Girardi) has a plan in mind. Maybe Ace matches up."

Aceves had never faced Kendrick, and Mathis was 0-for-2 with a strikeout against the right-hander before smacking his game-winning hit past Jerry Hairston Jr. and off the fence in left-center.

"I think it was a little slider or a cutter," Mathis said of the pitch he smoked.

Had the Yankees not wasted strong scoring chances in the second and fourth, Girardi's strategy wouldn't be on the back page of today's Post.

Derek Jeter hit Jered Weaver's third pitch of the game over the left-field fence, and Alex Rodriguez's blast to left opening the fourth staked Andy Pettitte to a 2–0 lead. But the Yankees had first and second and no outs in both the second and fourth innings and didn't score, with Robinson Cano, Nick Swisher and Melky Cabrera all failing in those situations.

"Not being able to get it done there is probably part of the reason we lost the game," Girardi said.

Johnny Damon upped the Yankees' bulge to 3–0 with a homer to right in the fifth, but the Angels copped a 4–3 lead on a solo homer by Kendrick, a two-run shot by Vladimir Guerrero and Maicer Izturis' sacrifice fly that scored Kendrick from third in the seventh. Jorge Posada tied the score, 4–4, in the eighth with a solo homer that could have been a two-run blast had pinch runner Brett Gardner not been caught trying to swipe second when the Angels pitched out.

"We have a lot of confidence in CC pitching, but we have to swing the bats better," said Jeter, who went 0-for-5 after the homer and stranded two runners in the eighth inning. "We had chances to score some runs with runners in scoring position."

The Yankees were 0-for-8 in the clutch. In the three ALCS games, they are 3-for-28 (.107) and hitless in their last 20 at-bats with runners in scoring position.

Having used Mariano Rivera for 2 ⅓ innings (25 pitches) in Game 2 on Saturday night, Girardi set a one-inning limit on his closer, and it was a wild frame.

Rivera entered after Mathis led off the 10th with a double. Rivera fielded Erick Aybar's bunt and had Mathis at third until he bounced a throw to Rodriguez that got by the third baseman.

With runners at the corners and the infield in, Chone Figgins hit a grounder to Mark Teixeira that he fielded for the first out. Bobby Abreu was walked intentionally. Rivera induced Torii Hunter and Guerrero to hit consecutive grounders to Teixeira to end the inning.

"When you lose, you look forward to tomorrow," Posada said, "and we have a pretty good guy on the mound." ■

Andy Pettitte worked into the seventh inning of Game 2, scattering seven hits that produced three runs. The bullpen failed to shut the door, however, and the Yankee bats also went cold.

Joe's maneuvers finally crap out

October 19, 2009 • By Mike Vaccaro

Well, this was bound to happen, wasn't it? Joe Girardi had spent his first five games as an October manager running from pitcher to pitcher, from move to move, as if he were a seven-year-old opening presents on Christmas morning. *Cool, an XBox! Awesome, Transformers! Yay, a new football! Wow, Damaso Marte!*

Time after time, game after game, Girardi seemed hell-bent on turning the Yankees into a Little League team, making sure everyone got to play every night. It was harrowing sometimes. It was breathtaking. And it had worked: every lever Girardi pulled, every button he pushed, every switch he flicked. All of it.

He rolled one seven after another.

But that's the problem playing dice, Jack. Eventually, the bones turn cold. Eventually, you take one too many brisk jogs out to the pitcher's mound, you scrawl one too many squiggly lines on your lineup card, you outsmart yourself once too often.

And eventually, for no good reason, you remove David Robertson from the 11th inning of a playoff game with two outs and nobody on. You spend a few mandatory moments in the dugout scanning charts and fiddling with numbers and doing calculations in your head. And, let's be honest: maybe you're also feeling a wee bit bullet proof by now.

So you make your seventh pitching change of the night.

"There were so many changes," Angels center fielder Torii Hunter soon crowed, "I thought it was a spring training game."

You bring in your eighth pitcher, Alfredo Aceves, and it feels like the game ends in about seven seconds: a single to Yankees slaughterer Howie Kendrick, a double to the heretofore muffle-batted Jeff Mathis, a 5–4 loss to the Angels that all but hands them party favors as you welcome them back into this American League Championship Series.

"We liked the matchup with Ace better," Girardi said stoically a bit later. "And it didn't work."

Up to that moment, Girardi was on a bigger roll than Mike McD at Teddy KGB's place. He'd brought Mariano Rivera in earlier than he wanted to an inning earlier, and Rivera got out of a bases-loaded, nobody-out jam. Girardi took the extreme step of surrendering his designated hitter in order to replace Johnny Damon's noodle arm in left with Jerry Hairston Jr.'s legit one.

It was a hell of a streak. But for the second straight day, and for the fourth time in six playoff games, you could hear Yankees fans muttering about Girardi's indulgence for over-managing. Funny, too: it used to drive people crazy that Joe Torre would make a move too few, would overwork the key members of his bullpen a bit too much.

Now, it is Girardi's time. It means all 25 men on the roster bring their time sheets to the office every day. It means whipping through relief pitchers at unconventional and sometimes uncomfortable times. It means crossing your fingers a lot and hoping stuff happens in between Alex Rodriguez moonshots.

"I was a little surprised when he came to get me," Robertson admitted later on, though he was quick to add, "but Ace has had a great year, and (Girardi) knows how to handle all of us."

Girardi had been rescued Saturday night in Game 2, when the Angels kicked the ball around in the 13th, and he was able to keep his emergency long man, Chad Gaudin, under cellophane. He wasn't going to have the same luck now, even if the Angels had done everything they could to keep themselves from winning the game.

So now Girardi enters a brave new phase of this job, and we will see how he responds to his first postseason loss, one that will surely give him a shortened bullpen with CC Sabathia going on short rest today. In many ways, his career as Yankees manager begins at 7:57 tonight.

"We've had contributions from a lot of guys all year," Girardi said, "and we've gotten where we are because they've always done their share for this club."

Mostly, that's what's happened this postseason, too. Just not last night.

Last night there was no joy in Yankville. Bones Girardi had crapped out. ■

Joe Girardi has become a familiar face for home plate umpires, unafraid to make as many pitching changes as he needs to get the job done. Usually his relievers come up strong; in Game 2, it may have been a case of one too many moves for the Yankees skipper.

CC, A-Rod push Bombers a win from Series

October 20, 2009 • By George A. King III

The Yankees are nine innings away from another World Series appearance, thanks to two guys who have never been there.

One day after being lambasted for the way he used the bullpen, Joe Girardi's decision to start CC Sabathia in Game 4 of the ALCS against the Angels last night on three days' rest made Girardi look smart.

That involved a small degree of thinking. Writing Alex Rodriguez' name in the cleanup spot was a no-brainer.

Sabathia and Rodriguez—with help from Johnny Damon and Melky Cabrera—drove the Yankees past the Angels, 10–1, in front of 45,160 at Angel Stadium.

The victory, marred by two blown calls by umpires, puts the Yankees in a commanding, 3–1 lead in the best-of-seven series that resumes tomorrow night when A.J. Burnett faces Angels ace John Lackey.

Working on short rest for the first time since last October, Sabathia proved to be worth the $161 million the Yankees dropped on him last December. In eight innings, he allowed a run, five hits, two walks and fanned five.

"I didn't feel any different at all," Sabathia said of the short rest. "This late in the season you are feeling healthy."

Long considered a player who was suffocated by the postseason attention and pressure, Rodriguez is shedding that label. He went 3-for-4, homered, drove in two runs, scored three and stole a base.

"I will say that in other postseasons I failed, sometimes miserably," said Rodriguez, who has hit five homers this postseason, one shy of Bernie Williams' club record. "It certainly feels good to come through for my team and help my team win."

Damon added a two-run homer in the eighth, and Cabrera went 3-for-4 and drove in four runs.

Through five innings Sabathia had given up a run and threw only 63 pitches. He allowed the first two Angels to reach leading off the sixth but induced Juan Rivera to bang into a 6–3 double play and watched Howie Kendrick's liner land in Mark Teixeira's glove, getting him back in a groove that saw him retire the last eight hitters he faced.

Since he started the postseason with a less than stellar October ledger, there were questions about Sabathia in the only month that counts in the Yankees' universe.

"I never had any doubt about me being able to perform on this stage and pitch well late in October, but it seems like people did," said Sabathia, who is 3–0 in three starts this postseason. "I feel great. Hopefully I can keep it going."

Angels starter Scott Kazmir against Sabathia wasn't a contest. Kazmir struggled with control and didn't get out of the fifth. In four-plus frames, he allowed four runs, six hits and three walks.

Teixeira, another Yankee who has never been to the World Series, didn't want to get too giddy about needing one win in three games to get there.

"This was a big win; we are one game away," said Teixeira, who singled in five at-bats. "We can't get ahead of ourselves. If you start thinking about the World Series, you are not going to get the job done."

Nobody who watched it will ever forget the 2004 ALCS against the Red Sox. The Yankees had four shots at winning one game and didn't.

Now, five years later, they have three to get one.

With Sabathia ready to pitch a Game 7 if needed and Rodriguez continuing to look like the biggest kid in Little League, you have to like the Yankees' chances of getting to the World Series for the first time since 2003. At least that's the way to bet. ∎

Starting on three days' rest did not bother CC Sabathia and helped exorcise some of Joe Girardi's demons. Sabathia pitched strong and got more support than he needed from the bats: 10 runs on 13 hits, punctuated by homers from Alex Rodriguez and Johnny Damon.

Alex rewriting legacy

October 20, 2009 • By Mike Vaccaro

In only 245 days, he has risen from pariah to messiah, from reviled to revered, from a rogue whose reputation was left stranded on the side of the road to a player who makes grown men shake their heads in wonder.

Eight months and three days from one kind of press conference—where Alex Rodriguez famously admitted he knew he hadn't been taking Tic Tacs—to another kind, where he all but had to swear that he really doesn't have X-ray vision, a bulletproof chest and the ability to fly.

"I've never had a streak like that," Nick Swisher marveled when this 10–1 Yankees romp was done, "but the ball has to look like a beach ball to him now. There are a lot of players who have played this game. I don't know any who did what he's done here."

It was simply another day at the October office for Rodriguez, another home run (his fifth of the postseason), another three hits (make that 11 in seven postseason games), another flawless day in the field.

If CC Sabathia made it clear that the Angels weren't going to seize whatever momentum they'd gained in Game 3, it was Rodriguez who turned that momentum upside-down.

Every day now, he not only puts a little bit more distance between himself and the lowest moment of his public life, he puts a bit more space between himself and the pressures that used to strangle and suffocate him.

"He needs to finish," Reggie Jackson, always the authority on October legitimacy, said, a reminder to A-Rod and to everyone else that the jackals won't be jettisoned forever until he slips a championship ring on his finger. And that may well be so.

Still, Rodriguez has done more than anyone to nudge the Yankees to the doorstep of a 40th American League pennant. When he is hitting as he is, when Sabathia is throwing as he is, there is little else to worry about.

Wretched umpiring can't harm them. Joe Girardi stays mostly planted on his seat in the dugout, his wheels silenced for a few hours.

Yet A-Rod understands the hole that still sits in the thick of his resume. Asked if his epic performance across this postseason will vanquish at last whatever questions remain about his autumnal fortitude, he admitted, "I'm not sure about that."

And added, with as much candor as we've ever seen from him: "I will say that in other postseasons I've failed and sometimes failed miserably."

Just not this postseason, not from the moment he launched a two-run haymaker of a home run off Minnesota's Joe Nathan in Game 2 of the Division Series, not when he drove a game-tying knife through the guts of the Angels in Game 2 of the ALCS, not at the end of Game 3 when he was given the Barry Bonds treatment, drawing an intentional walk with nobody on base.

"It's obvious he's brought his game onto the field, what he does during the season," said Angels manager Mike Scioscia, who is starting to look like Wile E. Coyote after each of these games, wondering if he'll ever figure out a way to get Road Runner out in a big situation. "He's been as clutch as anyone could have hoped for on their side."

Someone asked Rodriguez what this felt like, and he spoke about the game slowing down for him when he plays this way, about swinging the bat well, about seeing the ball well, about being patient and passing the baton and all the rest. The truth is, he's as new to all of this as the rest of us.

Which brings us, as it should, back to Reggie, who hit five homers in the 1977 playoffs, a mark A-Rod tied yesterday, one behind Bernie Williams' single-season record. Mr. October spoke of the special privilege it is to watch the likes of A-Rod, of Ryan Howard, of Albert Pujols, and his advice was simple.

"You want to enjoy it," Jackson said.

Watching the dizzying high Alex Rodriguez is riding, only 245 days after his nauseating low, how can you do anything but? ∎

With five homers in the first seven games of the postseason and a hit in every game of the playoffs, A-Rod left no doubt that he was holding the Yankees' hottest bat.

Series ticket on hold after wacky inning

October 22, 2009 • By George A. King III

A.J. Burnett placed them in a cavernous crater early. The trench Phil Hughes dug late wasn't as deep, but together the right-handed ditch diggers cost the Yankees a chance to punch a World Series ticket.

Burnett gave up four runs to the Angels before getting an out in the first and—after the Yankees rallied with six two-out runs in the top of the seventh—Hughes flushed a one-run lead in the bottom of the inning as the Yankees dropped a 7–6 decision in Game 5 of the ALCS last night in front of an Angel Stadium crowd of 45,113.

With the Yankees holding a 3–2 lead in the best-of-seven series, the action shifts to Yankee Stadium tomorrow night for Game 6, weather permitting.

"I feel I let the squad down, no doubt," said Burnett, who allowed six runs and eight hits in six-plus innings and ignited the seventh-inning rally by giving up a single to Jeff Mathis and walking Erick Aybar, the No. 9 hitter.

Because Burnett rebounded strongly from the disastrous first inning with five shutout frames, Joe Girardi stuck with Burnett, in another move that will be second-guessed.

"We talked about it, but he was throwing the ball so well," said Girardi, who noted Burnett's pitch count was at 80 going into the seventh. "We liked what we saw from him and stuck with him. If he's around 105 pitches, it's probably a different story."

The three runs in the seventh, when the Angels chased Burnett, saved Mike Scioscia from being fitted for goat's horns.

The Angels had to sweat lefty closer Brian Fuentes going through the heart of the Yankees' order in the ninth. Johnny Damon's liner to first was the initial out. Mark Teixeira lofted the first pitch to right for the second out. That set up Alex Rodriguez against Fuentes and, on orders from Scioscia, he intentionally walked the potential tying run to face Hideki Matsui.

With Freddy Guzman running for Rodriguez, Fuentes went to a full count on Matsui and walked him. Robinson Cano got plunked to load the bases for the ice-cold Nick Swisher.

Fuentes was ahead 0–2 and ran the count full before Swisher's miserable postseason continued with a pop-up to short left field.

"A big hit right there would have erased a lot," said Swisher, who is 3-for-29 (.103) in the postseason and 2-for-17 (.118) in the ALCS. "It's the biggest stage, and you want to come through there."

Thanks to a curious decision by the Angels' respected manager, the Yankees rallied from a 4–0 deficit in the seventh inning by scoring six runs after Scioscia lifted ace John Lackey for lefty Darren Oliver.

Scioscia had Lackey (104 pitches) on the mound with the bases loaded, two outs and a 4–0 lead when he shockingly hooked the right-hander and brought in Oliver to face the switch-hitting, and frigid, Teixeira, who was 2-for-3 lifetime against Oliver and 0-for-1 with a walk in the series.

"You are always glad to see Lackey leave the game," said Teixeira, who rocked a first-pitch slider for a three-run double that ignited a six-run rally and included an RBI single by Matsui and a two-run Cano triple.

After Burnett gave up a single to Mathis and walked Aybar, Girardi brought in lefty Damaso Marte to face the switch-hitting Chone Figgins. His bunt advanced the runners a base each. Bobby Abreu's anemic grounder to the right side scored Mathis from third, sent Aybar to third and brought Hughes in to face Torii Hunter.

He walked on five pitches, and Hughes gave up an RBI single to Vladimir Guerrero on a 1–2 pitch that tied the score, 6–6.

Hughes fell behind Kendry Morales before the switch-hitter laced a single to right that plated Hunter and gave the hosts a 7–6 lead.

Which turned out to be just enough to get the ALCS back to The Bronx. ∎

In a strange contest, it was one hole too many for the Yankees to climb out of. Phil Hughes and A.J. Burnett struggled to get their best stuff going in the later innings, allowing the Angels to back into a win that lifted their spirits heading back to New York.

Pettitte, Bombers clinch return to Series

October 25, 2009 • By George A. King III

When it comes to possessing a thirst for winning World Series, the apple didn't fall far from the Steinbrenner tree. Instead, it hugged the bark on the way down.

Not long after Derek Jeter poured a river of Chandon champagne over him and his sister, Jennifer Steinbrenner Swindal, Hal Steinbrenner showed while he might not have the bluster his pop had, the son has similar needs.

"We expect to win a championship," Hal, the Yankees' managing general partner, said after the Yankees punched their ticket to the World Series against the Phillies that opens Wednesday in The Bronx by handing the bumbling Angels a 5–2 loss in Game 6 of the ALCS last night at Yankee Stadium.

So, with their eyes stinging and their heads on the way to a monster hangover, the Yankees were presented with the final challenge of what so far has been a magical 2009 season.

The champagne flowed freely and reminded Hal and Jennifer of the days when Jeter would soak The Boss in the bubbly. "He used to do this to my Dad, I guess it's my turn," Hal said as he reached for a towel.

After six seasons outside the World Series, the Yankees are back. Armed with a superior rotation, bullpen, having four of the possible seven games slated for Yankee Stadium and a smoking Alex Rodriguez, the Yankees are 2-to-1 favorites to cop their 27th World Championship.

They spent an ocean of money on younger arms, but Andy Pettitte, who had to swallow a colossal pay cut, lifted the Yankees past the Angels.

When the Yankees put Pettitte's plaque in Monument Park the inscription will read: "He pitched and won a lot of big games." The Yankees begged the 37-year-old lefty to beat the Angels for two reasons. One, a win would send the Yankees to the World Series.

Two, by avoiding a Game 7, the Yankees could set up their rotation against the Phillies in the Series and would have ace CC Sabathia, who was named the ALCS MVP for going 2–0, ready to hurl the opener. Carve two more notches in Pettitte's impressive pinstriped belt after the veteran lefty delivered.

Pettitte, whose 38 starts are a postseason record, passed John Smoltz for the all-time lead in wins with 16. His seven LCS victories are second to Dave Stewart's record of eight. In 6 ⅓ innings Pettitte, who will participate in his eighth World Series (seventh as a Yankee), allowed a run and seven hits.

"He did what he has done his whole career," Jeter said of Pettitte. Joba Chamberlain replaced Pettitte after Juan Rivera dumped a soft, one-out single into right field in the seventh. Chamberlain stranded the runner by inducing two ground balls and preserved a 3–1 lead. With the two-run cushion, manager Joe Girardi summoned Mariano Rivera for a six-out save and the top of the Angels' lineup due up. Rivera gave up a run in the eighth on Vladimir Guerrero's two-out, RBI single, but posted his postseason record 37th save by getting the final three outs.

"I didn't think anything of it," Rivera said of being asked for two innings. "I just wanted to get them out as quickly as I could."

The Angels made it easier for Rivera by committing two errors on sacrifice bunts in the eighth that fueled a two-run run rally and included a sacrifice fly by Mark Teixeira.

It was the first postseason earned run at home allowed by Rivera since Oct. 22, 2000 (26 games), in Game 2 against the Mets.

"We left a lot of guys (12) on base," said Johnny Damon, whose two-run single highlighted a three-run fourth inning that erased a 1–0 lead. "But we came through."

And stand four wins away from feeding the same beast in Hal Steinbrenner. ∎

At the end of Game 6, all seemed right with the world. Derek Jeter was soaking everyone in champagne, the Yankees were celebrating, and the team was on its way into the final stretch in pursuit of a 27th world title.

One Mo time: Rivera closes out ALCS win

October 25, 2009 • By Mark Hale

Once again, Mariano Rivera was center stage for a crucial Yankees victory. And once again, he shut the door on their opponents.

This time, Rivera got the final six outs of a 5–2 victory over the Angels that sent the Bombers to their 40th American League pennant and a meeting with the Phillies in the World Series.

"Six big outs," Jorge Posada said of Rivera's two innings of work in Game 6 of the ALCS.

Although Rivera, the greatest postseason closer of all time, gave up a run in the eighth inning, he still finished the

Angels off, striking out Gary Matthews Jr. swinging to end the series.

It was the 13th time Rivera has gotten a two-inning save in the postseason.

"The plan was, if we needed him for two (innings) tonight, he was fresh and ready to go," pitching coach Dave Eiland said. "And it worked out to where we needed him for two or we could use him for two. And he went out there, and he got the job done."

Rivera said he was not concerned with the Yankees asking him to pitch two innings, adding he had "no doubts."

"That doesn't work in my agenda," he said.

Rivera saw his postseason scoreless streak end at 16 innings when he served up a run in the eighth inning on Vladimir Guerrero's RBI single. It marked the first time Rivera had given up an earned run in the playoffs since Game 1 of the 2005 ALDS.

In the ninth inning, though, he set the Angels down 1-2-3.

"We know we had a couple days off in between, and we've got a couple days off in between here and the World Series," Posada said. "So you can't say enough about Mariano. Mariano gave us a chance every time, and nobody's like him. There's nobody like him."

Rivera will now go for his fifth World Series championship and first since 2000. In his Fall Classic career, he has pitched 20 games, allowing just four earned runs in 31 innings for a 1.16 ERA. ∎

Despite giving up his first postseason run since 2005, Mariano Rivera was all smiles after his six-out save punched the Yankees' ticket to their first World Series in six years.

Andy dandy in postseason again

October 25, 2009 • By Joel Sherman

Andy Pettitte was the lone figure on the field at Yankee Stadium early Saturday night. The lights were off and a strong rain was falling. Game 6 of the ALCS had been postponed about an hour earlier. Pettitte now had a huge workday ahead of him in 24 hours, but he ran and ran on a doused warning track.

And that felt right: Pettitte working hard in October.

For now this can be said about Pettitte: when it comes to the postseason, no pitcher has ever started more games, won more often and won more clinching games. Sure Pettitte has benefited from pitching for superb teams and in an era with three rounds of playoffs. But it is one thing to have opportunity. Another to capitalize.

And, of course, one reason the Yankees have enjoyed all this success is because they have had Pettitte to pitch so often in the playoffs. There will be many lasting images of this time in Yankees history. One of the most enduring will be Pettitte, the cap pulled low on his forehead, his glove held high, covering everything but his dark eyes.

Often at this time of year, this has looked like victory. It did again last night.

"He really is a big-game pitcher," Jorge Posada said. "He really is amazing."

Pettitte further galvanized his rep in ALCS Game 6. For he not only won, but he won when a loss would have been so debilitating, when a loss would have meant using CC Sabathia in the decisive contest and harming World Series chances even if the Yankees prevailed.

Pettitte kept Sabathia in line for Game 1 against the Phillies by limiting the Angels to one run in 6⅓ innings in a 5–2 triumph that sent the Yankees to their 40th World Series. Pettitte is going to his eighth Series, seventh as a Yankee, and considering Philadelphia's lefty might, he projects as pretty darn vital again.

In a euphoric clubhouse roiled by champagne, beer, blaring music and hearty hugs, Hal Steinbrenner called Pettitte "the best investment I made all year long." And that was even with $423.5 million earmarked for Sabathia, A.J. Burnett and Mark Teixiera. At the end of a tough negotiation, Pettitte accepted a major pay cut, down to $5.5 million plus incentives. It felt like a dismissive afterthought.

"Everybody knows I wasn't really happy with the contract I took," Pettitte said.

"But I wanted to take it to come back here to have a chance to do this."

So he did this: won his 16th playoff game, eclipsing John Smoltz. Generated his fifth clinching win, topping Roger Clemens, Catfish Hunter and Dave Stewart. And he did it in style, producing his 14th postseason start in which he yielded one or no earned runs.

To prepare for this moment, Pettitte began running under the Tampa sun in February and continued in a late October deluge in New York because, he said, "I stick to my routine; I run before I start."

So he had the endurance when the biggest out of Game 6 was needed. Two outs, two runners in scoring position, Yankees up by two, 3–1 in the sixth. Pettitte fell behind Kendry Morales 3–0. A walk and Joba Chamberlain would be in the game. A hit and the score would be tied. Pettitte told himself not to give in. He threw a fastball for a strike and then a hard sinker. Morales smacked the ball back toward the mound. In a goalie reflex, Pettitte swatted the ball down with his glove, retrieved, threw to first. Crisis averted, lead preserved.

"That is what we expect of Andy, especially in games like this," pitching coach Dave Eiland said.

And the Yankees got it, again. Pettitte left with one out in the seventh to a standing roar from the largest crowd ever at the new Stadium, 50,173. A cheer for today but also for all the previous October heavy lifting.

"I didn't want to put it on CC," Pettitte said. "I didn't want him to have to pitch a Game 7."

There is no Game 7. Cap low, glove high: it looked like October victory in The Bronx again. ■

Andy Pettitte is perhaps the best starting pitcher in postseason history, though he seemed little more than an afterthought heading into the year. Still, when it was time for the Yankees to get a quality start in a clinching game, it was the aging lefty who took the mound for a record-breaking appearance.